This is a series of books about jazz artists, all of whom have made either a significant contribution or have had an impact on the jazz scene. Unlike some jazz books that concentrate upon the detail of the performers' lives or music, this series is concerned with much more. Here can be seen the social background into which the subject was born and raised and the environment in which his or her music was formed. The social, domestic, racial and commercial pressures that shaped the person are examined alongside an assessment of other musicians who may have influenced the artist or been influenced by them. Of course, the music is not overlooked and each book carries a discographical essay in which the artist's recorded output is summarized and analyzed. Well-illustrated, the Life & Times series of books is an important and long overdue addition to jazz literature.

Dizzy Gillespie

HIS
LIFE & TIMES

BARRY McRAE

Omnibus Press
LONDON/SYDNEY/COLOGNE

REMEMBERING SINCLAIR TRAILL

First published in hardback in 1988 in UK by
SPELLMOUNT LTD.
12 Dene Way, Speldhurst,
Tunbridge Wells, Kent TN3 0NX

This edition published in 1988 in UK by
OMNIBUS PRESS
(A Division of Book Sales Limited)

ISBN 0-7119-1441-9
Order No. OP 44635

Exclusive Distributors:
Book Sales Limited
8/9 Frith Street, London W1V 5TZ, UK
Omnibus Press
GPO Box 330, Sydney, NSW 2001, Australia

To the Music Trade only:
Music Sales Limited
8/9 Frith Street, London W1V 5TZ, UK

Designed by: Words & Images,
Speldhurst, Tunbridge Wells, Kent
Typeset by: Vitaset,
Paddock Wood, Kent
Printed & bound in Great Britain by
Anchor Brendon Ltd., Tiptree, Essex

CONTENTS

ACKNOWLEDGEMENTS

I would like to say a special thanks to David Redfern and Photo Chadel, Verve Records, Ben Baird, Hervé Derrien, Susanna Schapowalow, Bernard Long, Hans Harzheim, Howard Lucraft, George Gilmore and Harvé Derrier whose photographs enhance the book. Thanks also to Tony Middleton whose vast discographical mind was put to its usual impressive use in the biographical essay. I would also like to express my gratitude to Graham Fowler for the loan of certain records and acknowledge the invaluable assistance of such important books as Leonard Feather's *Encyclopedia Of Jazz*, Feather and Ira Gitler's *Encyclopedia of Jazz in the Seventies* and John Chilton's *Who's Who Of Jazz*. Finally, I would like to say a special thanks to my wife Sylvia who gave valuable editorial advice and put the whole manuscript through our word processor.

Although efforts have been made to trace the present copyright holders of photographs, the publishers apologise in advance for any unintentional omission or neglect and will be pleased to insert the appropriate acknowledgement to companies or individuals in any subsequent edition of this book.

INTRODUCTION

Dizzy Gillespie's status as master of his instrument has never been in doubt. His virtuoso performances in the halycon days of bebop place him alongside Charlie Parker, Thelonious Monk, Bud Powell and Kenny Clarke as one of the pioneers of the new music. As a trumpeter he was to be one of the most outstanding players in jazz history, but he was also a composer, arranger, singer and conga drummer of distinction. Not all of these skills were paraded in his earlier days but he was under twenty and already a fine musician when he joined Teddy Hill's Band in New York in 1937.

Two years in the big band of Cab Calloway were followed by spells with other leaders including Lucky Millinder, Charlie Barnet and Benny Carter. There was even a brief stay with Duke Ellington in 1943 but, by this time, he had begun to earn a reputation as a musical experimentalist in the emerging modern jazz, bebop. In 1944 he joined Billy Eckstine and, for the first time, was able to enlarge on his earlier experience and show himself to be a highly original arranger. Several players involved in the new music were in the band, men such as Wardell Gray, Dexter Gordon and Art Blakey, but it was in activities away from the band in which Gillespie really excelled.

In 1945, it was the small group recordings that established his pre-eminent position amongst the small coterie of musicians set on changing the face of jazz. These records set the real standards as Gillespie, Parker and their colleagues laid down the ground rules of bop. They took jazz away from melodic variation and paraphrase. The chord sequence became the backbone on which the style was built, and both men showed how effortlessly they could build new tunes on them. Gone was the old concept of improvisation as Gillespie played a vital part in the construction of a whole new musical edifice and in the formulation of a vernacular required to express it.

His experience with Eckstine had made him realise that small group bop could be adapted to an orchestral format and, in 1945, he formed his first big band. Unfortunately, its life was short but, in the following year, he reformed and the new aggregation enjoyed artistic and commercial success in disproportionate degrees until 1950.

Ironically, it was not the precision of the section work, the creative brilliance of the solos nor the superb swing generated by the band that, at first, attracted the audiences. There was more interest in the leader's racy, off-beat singing with its onomatopoeic believability. Still, cynics had some justification in suggesting that fringe listeners went further and were even more impressed by Gillespie's eccentric dress and his on-stage antics than they were by the singing that, like his trumpet, was full of rhythmic daring, creative logic and sheer excitement.

For his part, Gillespie believed passionately in his music and he was prepared to use almost any means available to spread its popularity. He certainly accepted that the visual impact was important and saw nothing wrong in the fact that his horn-rimmed shades, goatee beard and beret became the uniform for the larger-than-life bopper and that the fans followed suit.

Having his own band was an asset to Gillespie the composer; he had a band to exploit his own fine writing, and compositions like *Things to Come, Salt Peanuts, Ool-Ya-Koo, Manteca* and *Night in Tunisia* were regularly performed. During this period, he also became enamoured with the fusion of Cuban music and jazz, producing a musical alloy christened 'cubop'. Conga master Chano Pozo actually played in Gillespie's band for some time and was induced to give instructions to his leader in the difficult art of playing his instrument.

After 1950, Gillespie returned to combo leading with groups that included pianist Wade Legge, saxophonist Bill Graham and singer Joe Carroll. Highly successful European tours were undertaken in 1952 and 1953, but not long after his return he joined Norman Granz's Jazz at the Philharmonic package. He had appeared briefly with them in the forties but there was now greater commitment, and he recorded for Granz's own record label until the owner sold out in 1960.

Little persuasion was required by the State Department to induce Gillepie's return to the role of big band leader and, in 1956, he took an impressive unit on tours including the Middle East and South America. These goodwill excursions were successful on all fronts, but the musical climate in America was still not right and, on returning home, he settled for parading his solo talents in the JATP arena.

Throughout the sixties Gillespie toured extensively with his own small groups, but he never missed the chance to work on record with a full orchestra. It was sometimes claimed that he was coasting, but this was rarely born out on record. In fact, he rejoined Norman Granz in 1974 and the Pablo label gave his career a considerable fillip. A series of outstanding records appeared and they found him in the company of men such as Joe Pass, Roy Eldridge, Oscar Peterson and also with the excellent big band led by Machito.

In the eighties Gillespie remained a consistently important instrumental voice on the world tour. The New York, Monterey and Montreux festivals were like second homes and, if the great man did protect his chops by playing congas and singing during his programme, it was understandable. In October 1987, he was seventy years old and, although there were increasing examples of his taking things a little easy on stage, when the mood was right and the challenge sufficient, he could cross trumpets with the finest of the new guard.

CHAPTER 1

THINGS TO COME

The town of Cheraw stands on the Pee Dee River in Chesterfield County, South Carolina. As befits a town in one of the 'British' states, it was settled in the mid eighteenth century by the Welsh and even today boasts, as one of its finest old buildings, St David's Episcopal Church (1773). Like most of the area, it also contains its array of antebellum mansions, but it has never been without those less privileged.

In 1917, 50% of the U.S. population could still be classified as rural and it was into this situation that John Birks Gillespie was born on 21 October. It was the year that Woodrow Wilson asked Congress for a declaration of war against the Central Powers and, within months of Gillespie's birth, the Eighteenth (dry) Amendment was passed by Congress as a prelude to the 1920 Volstead Act and prohibition.

None of this would have impressed Mama Lottie Gillespie as she brought a ninth child into an already extremely poor family. Only seven lived to be named, but Papa James Gillespie had to work at two jobs to support his family. During the week he was a bricklayer and at weekends he would play piano and lead his own band. As a man, he was something of an enigma; he treated his wife well, at times buying presents that he could not afford. He also bailed out the musicians in his band with small loans, although this was made more essential by the fact that he kept all of the instruments at the family home, to prevent them from hocking them.

He was, however, extremely cruel to the children. On most Sunday mornings the boys in the family would be whipped almost as a preparation for what they might do wrong. John Birks certainly resented this and even at an early age was something of a rebel. He built up a healthy mistrust of his fellow man and, even at school, was often featured in the skirmish-of-the-day.

What did occupy his mind more constructively were the

instruments around the house. He began to experiment with them surreptitiously and he became acquainted with the 'feeling' and sound of certain of them. This interest followed him into school and he volunteered for the school band despite the fact that his lack of seniority weighed against him when instruments were given out. He finally got a trombone and decided to put some work into investigating its mysteries.

Fortunately for posterity, he was sidetracked by a neighbour's son who had been given a trumpet as a Christmas gift. Gillespie invited himself into the process of mastering the new beast and, by the time he was twelve, was probably the only person in town who could play both trumpet and trombone. Sadly, his father had died when he was only ten, so he never lived to hear his youngest on his first choice horn.

There were far more important matters to concern Gillespie at the time. 1929 had seen the Wall Street Crash and, by 1930, due to the one crop system and the boll weevil of blues legend, almost one hundred million acres of the South had been hopelessly lost or seriously impaired by erosion. The result was that even more people were exposed to crushing poverty, and the Gillespies, poor when the main bread winner was alive, now faced serious financial trouble.

Franklin D. Roosevelt came to power in March 1932 and soon introduced his New Deal. He was genuinely in touch with the country he governed and was, in fact, the first president to use the radio in order to reach the people. Gillespie had left school in 1933 and he went on one of Roosevelt's public works' road gangs as a labourer. Manual work was not to his liking, however, and, almost at once, he quit.

The WPA (Works Progress Adminstration) began in the thirties and, during its eight-year life, was responsible for 650,000 miles of roads, 125,000 public buildings and the employment of 8,500,000 individuals. It also brought about something of a cultural revolution: turning American classical composers, writers and painters toward their own national heritage – genuine arts for, and about, the people.

Sadly, this did not include jazz although, in many ways, this was predictable. As an art music, jazz was at its lowest ebb, using as its crutch the misguided sentimentality of the music hall and, in the main, relying for its survival on its functional value to the dance hall. Nevertheless, the WPA did encourage artists and they were free to do what they wanted. It was indeed fortunate that most chose to document life in their homeland and, in so doing, provide an unsentimental documentary of its tribulations in the thirties.

At the time, young Gillespie saw the more functional side of WPA activities. He was all too conversant with its pay queues and seeing his brothers collecting their money, and the sight of them marking an X because they could not write made a lasting impression upon him. It certainly made more attractive the prospect of earning a living from music.

His first lucky break came in the summer of 1933 when the sixteen year old was invited to play trumpet at Laurinburg Technical Institute, a school for farming in North Carolina. It was a move that involved him in some study in agricultural methods, introduced him to the school football team but, more importantly, gave him time to expand his musical knowledge. He studied theory and found the piano a useful tool in his studies. Piano playing was a skill that he would turn to his advantage in later years, and there were times at Laurinburg when he divided his practice almost equally between trumpet and piano.

At weekends he began to play at parties and local dances and was even offered a job with King Oliver, who was passing through and in need of a trumpeter. The name meant nothing to Gillespie and he declined the offer, preferring to stay with the musicians he knew and still regarding himself as rather young to take such a chance.

He had, however, become somewhat disenchanted with school and the prospect of the obligatory manual work that was part of the curriculum. His family had moved north to Philadelphia during his stay at Laurinburg and, when the opportunity presented itself, he 'dropped out' of school and followed.

The family home was at 7th and Vine in South Philadelphia and Gillespie has described it as a 'hole in the ground'. This it was not, but the trumpeter was somewhat surprised when he visited the area in the seventies, 'that was the ghetto but they sent all the black people out . . . now it's all elegant town houses,' he mused.

Nevertheless, the 1935 musical scene in Philadelphia was healthy and Gillespie took several small-time jobs. He was ambitious to play in a big band, however, and later that year he joined Frankie Fairfax, one of the leading black bands in the district. His progress in the band was rapid, his playing had become very assured and he was well liked by the other sidemen. This popularity was helped while on tour in Charlotte, North Carolina when he saved the life of fellow trumpeter Fats Palmer, overcome by gas in his hotel room. For his part, Palmer's place in the Gillespie saga was assured because he was the man who dubbed John Birks, 'Dizzy', the sobriquet he enjoys to the present day.

Shortly after Gillespie had joined Fairfax, changes in the trumpet section had introduced Charlie Shavers and Bama Warwick to the band. Shavers, in particular, shared the youngster's interest in Roy Eldridge, and they became friends. Shavers had mastered many of 'Little Jazz's' favourite solos and he

Roy Eldridge

helped Gillespie to play them. This finally led to a little tension between them but did not destroy their relationship, and it was Shavers who persuaded Gillespie to make the big step, to join Lucky Millinder in New York.

In the event, he did not get the job, but decided to remain in New York. He could stay with his brother who was livng there, and soon he began to inhabit after-hours jam sessions and to get the Dizzy Gillespie name known. He also sat in with several name bands at the Savoy, including the Savoy Sultans, Willie Bryant and Chick Webb. This writer once heard Gillespie describe the Sultans as the 'most swinging band he ever heard' but the significant point was that he was easily holding his own in fast company.

14

The Savoy had become something of a spiritual home for Gillespie and it was at 'The Track', as it became known among musicians, that he met Teddy Hill. It was 1937 and the tenor playing leader was looking for a trumpeter to take on tour to Europe. Who better than the young man who sounded like his former sideman Roy Eldridge and could play many of the same licks?

Still short of his twentieth birthday, Gillespie accepted but, before going on the trip, went into the Bluebird Studio with the band and made his recording debut. To draw any firm conclusions on the basis of a nineteen year old's first recording session would be fatuous but, considered in the light of his activities in Philadelphia, his solo on *King Porter Stomp* is not without significance. While with Fairfax, he had sometimes put in voluntary rehearsal time alone, working things out on the *piano*. In his own words, he explained that 'I'd play chord changes, inverting them and substituting different notes, trying to see how different sounds led naturally, sometimes surprisingly, into others. I'd take them and play them on my horn, and used to surprise people with new combinations.'

Nothing in the way of harmonic licence is evident in the *King Porter Stomp* solo, but its rhythmic balance is, at least, unorthodox. The first four bars are like a typical Eldridge opening, as indeed are the third four bars. Where the difference occurs is in the off centre note placement in the second four and again in the final four. Perhaps even unrealised by the young man who was playing them, they give a distant hint of the angularity that was to become the norm for the music that was to evolve into bebop.

Such theories aside, Gillespie's competent reading and his sixteen bars of assured soloing were enough for Hill and, despite some opposition from older musicians within the band, the young trumpeter boarded the *Ile de France* for the trip of his lifetime!

The whole entourage was called The Cotton Club Show and the tour included London, Paris and Dublin. At the time, Gillespie resented his omission from the freelance recording sessions that took place in Paris and included his fellow bandsmen, Dickie Wells, Bill Dillard and Shad Collins. For some reason, he held Wells responsible for this state of affairs but, in reality, it is difficult to see how the trombonist could be blamed. The sessions were set up by the fiercely conservative Hughes Panassié. He had originally wanted Eldridge, who had not made the trip, and it would not be unreasonable to assume that he would have had reservations about a man who was barely twenty and with only one recording session under his belt.

Gillespie got his consolation in the whorehouses of the city and from the fact that he was earning $70.00 a week, a considerable sum at the time. After six weeks in Paris, the party moved on to London for a month's stay. There were no recording opportunities there but, after the nightly show at London's Palladium, the youngster frequently joined the town's after-hours jam session scene.

Union trouble over the three-month waiting time for an 'overseas' musician blighted his return to the States, but he had his mind on other things. Even in his earliest days of adulthood, Gillespie had been very much a 'ladies man'. The move to New York and his increasing fame had made it easier for him to pursue this interest, and he was rarely seen without a female companion on his arm.

There always seemed to be available women but, with characteristic human perversity, he began to lose interest in the camp followers. While still waiting for his union membership, he played an illicit gig with Edgar Hayes. It took him to Washington and, while there, he met a dancer called Lorraine. She had married young but had lost her first husband with a brain tumour. She was attractive and somewhat retiring and had little interest in hitting the night spots after a gruelling evening's work. Gillespie contacted her through notes passed by another dancer but, for her part, she was suspicious of his 'Dizzy' reputation. Finally, she relented and began 'seeing' the young trumpeter on a permanent basis.

On the musical front, things had also improved. The union card came through and Gillespie rejoined Hill. Kenny Clarke had joined the band on drums and another piece in the future bebop jigsaw had fallen into place. The leader was not totally enamoured of Clarke's 'bomb dropping', as he termed it, but it struck the right note in the ears of the band's young trumpet star. Whereas Hill was disconcerted by what he heard as the persistent Klook mop, Klook mop, Gillespie saw it as a way ahead. He pointed out that 'he drops his bombs on the fourth beat, and it leads over, the rhythm still going. That's the new way.' At least for a short time Gillespie had his way, Clarke remained in the band and, in the process, acquired the name 'Klook'.

However, just as the band began to get together, they lost some important bookings and split up. Hill himself gave up playing and, although it was hardly significant in 1939, became the booking manager at Minton's Playhouse. Amongst the first musicians whom he booked to play there were Kenny Clarke, Joe Guy and Thelonious Monk, and this was later to prove an important club in the evolution of bebop.

Gillespie was not out of work for long and, through Klook, he joined Edgar Hayes, this time as a regular member of the band. Unfortunately, the money was not good and, assisted by trumpeter

16

Mario Bauza, he got to try out with Cab Calloway. The circumstances were somewhat confused; without Calloway's prior knowledge Gillespie depped for Bauza in the band. He merely put on the uniform and sat in. He played well on the night, the leader liked what he heard and Gillespie was invited to join the band. It was a stay that was to last for two years and perhaps more than any other experience up to that time, established the trumpeter, not only as a completely self confident performer but also as a man who really did have a reputation in the 'business'! The Cab Calloway Orchestra traded in class, the pay was good, the uniforms were immaculate and the touring show had a superb chorus line with sixteen girls. Touring as the Cotton Club Show, the band used private rail cars or chartered buses.

Gillespie joined in August 1939 and almost immediately had his

Dizzy with Louis Armstrong and Lionel Hampton

first taste of an all-star-group. Master vibraphonist Lionel Hampton's recording contract with RCA Victor had worked out well for both parties. Featuring the dramatic skills of trumpeter Ziggy Elman, Hampton's powerful band had made records that enjoyed genuine, commercial success. On the strength of these, he had used certain sessions to record with players merely because he liked to work with them, and, in the course of three years, men such as Henry Allen, J.C. Higginbotham, Buster Bailey and selected Duke Ellington sidemen took part in such sessions.

Hampton had first heard Gillespie playing at the Apollo in New York and had been immediately impressed by his forward-looking style. Here was a young man ideally suited to one of his special sessions, and Hampton invited the youngster to join such giants as Coleman Hawkins, Charlie Christian, Benny Carter and Gillespie's colleague from the Calloway band, Chu Berry.

The outcome was totally successful, but attention must centre on a vibraphone showcase called *Hot Mallets*. Here for the first time on record the jazz world was to hear Gillespie moving some distance from the parent Eldridge style. After a routine drum and piano introduction, Gillespie takes what amounts to a cadenza

18

slightly separated from the main performance. It opens with a paraphrase of *Dancing Cheek to Cheek* and progresses through sixteen bars of ladder-climbing arpeggios including one that, in retrospect, could have been called pure bebop. He later returns for an eight-bar break that culminates in a similarly off-centre and 'boppish' run.

Certainly, Hampton took that view and, even to this day, has consistently claimed that this 1939 performance was the first recorded example of the new music. In view of parallel happenings in Kansas, one must be guarded about such sweeping assertions, but there is a genuine case for claiming that this Gillespie display in 1939 was as far along the path toward bebop as were Charlie Parker's 1940 solos with Jay McShann.

The young Kansas City altoist was still largely infuenced by tenor saxophonist Lester Young at that time but, as air shots from Station KFBI, Wichita, Kansas, show, Parker was also something of a chameleon. In the McShann orchestra's tour of the South and Midwest, they had stopped over to do a show for KFBI radio. In it Parker had responded to the material available and, while following the basic Young route through *Lady Be Good* approached *Body and Soul* more as might Coleman Hawkins.

Whatever the conclusion about the two men at this stage of development, Calloway was initially miffed by his own sideman's gratuitously taken leave of absence. Luckily, his attitude to this practice did mellow, but he had always been a strict disciplinarian. In a Tribute To Duke Ellington TV show, he related his story of briefly taking over the leadership of the Ellington Band only to be appalled by the casual approach of its members. Perhaps, because of this, he also resented his own musicians' playing in after-hours jam sessions. It was a practice that was extremely attractive to the men concerned, but it could be argued that it blunted their enthusiasm for their main job.

Gillespie certainly ignored his leader's feelings on the subject. He resented being left out of Calloway's band-within-a-band 'the Cab Jivers' and sought out small-group sessions at Minton's Playhouse and at Clark Monroe's Uptown House. Such places brought him into contact with, among others, Hill's house pianist Thelonious Monk and quite an amount of his early jamming involved his own keyboard skills and led to an interchange of ideas with Monk.

Inevitably, the discipline of the big band with its three man trumpet section restricted Gillespie's more flamboyant playing. Within the band, he tended to remain loyal to his Eldridge-based style with its quirky overtones. His two intense choruses on the 1940 *Bye Bye Blues* show how well he could do his big-band showboating, and this suited Calloway ideally.

Charlie Parker

Gillespie himself felt that his final divorce from the Eldridge influence occurred at this time, but this title and other recorded evidence suggests that it is more realistic to see the Calloway period as something of a stylistic dichotomy. In his band role Gillespie was perfecting the style that was related to the big band tradition but, in other circumstances, he was allowing himself the licence to explore the outer frontiers of his music.

Fortunately, Calloway realised that Gillespie's interests extended beyond being merely an instrumentalist and that he was ready to flex his muscles as an arranger. He had no violent objections to this and, in fact, encouraged the young trumpeter to submit charts for the band. At this stage, Gillespie was imaginative without being radical but, as a title like *Pickin' the Cabbage* shows, he could make use of the available licence. The result was an arrangement, influenced by the methods of the day, but with something of his own musical personality added.

The Calloway band continued to tour and, while in Kansas, Gillespie met Charlie Parker. Their 1940 meeting, engineered by trumpeter Buddy Anderson was an event that was to change jazz history. At first, they were somewhat wary of each other; at their first jam session Gillespie actually played piano, and neither had any reason to believe that their relationship would develop further.

Gillespie had more important things on his mind at the time. He had married Lorraine and, in addition to the normal problems of adjustment, the newlyweds had to face the inconvenience involved in having no permanent address and, at first, of both working unsocial hours. Nevertheless, things worked out well and, despite being somewhat less than rich, Gillespie proved to be a generous husband, and at least they had no family with which to cope.

They were never to have children and never really missed them. Lorraine has said, 'Had God wanted me to have children, I woulda had plenty of them.' The main thing was that the Gillespies had a great deal of respect for each other and the absence of family was never an issue for them.

The young trumpeter's stay with Calloway ended in a dramatic manner. During the course of a stage performance, there was an incident in which missiles were thrown about on stage. Based on his previous and frequent misdemeanours, Gillespie was the obvious choice as the culprit. Calloway did not hesitate to accuse him, and in the altercation that followed, Gillespie pulled a knife. His leader was cut, Gillespie was paid off and, together with his wife, returned to New York and greater job availability.

CHAPTER 2

UP ON TEDDY'S HILL

The return to New York meant that Gillespie was on hand to return to the jam sessions that were taking place at Minton's Playhouse and Monroe's Uptown House. These were becoming increasingly important to the young trumpeter and were beginning to shape his musical development.

In fact, he was never employed at either establishment and his playing there, in contravention of local musician's rules, was always on the basis of 'sitter in'. With Monk and Clarke in the house band at Minton's and Parker, for a time, at least an official member of the Monroe's clique, Gillespie was in his element.

One thing that both rooms had in common was that, although they were prepared to provide food for the visiting 'jammers', nobody except the resident musicians actually got paid. They relied on the fact that, owing to the attraction of the workshop atmosphere they were fostering, jazz musicians were more than willing to play for nothing. They were in fact, extremely jealous of the privilege and began to evolve an exclusion system that was based mainly on musical ability but that was certainly not above an element of racial discrimination.

Trumpeter Johnny Carisi and trombonist Kai Winding were two white musicians accepted in the sessions but, in the main, both Minton's and Monroe's were effectively 'black' clubs. In truth, it must be said that technical facility was the ultimate criterion and that Carisi and Winding were accepted only because they could survive in the creative hothouse that was generated week after week.

In contrast, there were posers of all races who sought to attract attention by getting on stage without the musical technique to compete. They were normally given their chance but gradually systems were devised by the regular habitués to ensure that incompetents were frozen off. Crippling tempos took care of most

Big Sid Catlett

rhythm section aspirants, while difficult keys were introduced to deter keyboard and horn hopefuls. Standard tunes would be given subtle harmonic variations and the new changes would stump all but the most sophisticated musical mind.

Apart from Gillespie, the trumpet regulars included Hot Lips Page, Joe Guy and Freddie Webster. Saxophonists Don Byas and Kermit Scott would join Parker, while pianists Sir Charles Thompson, Bud Powell, Kenny Kersey and Pee Wee Tinney would compete for Monk's piano chair. Amongst the bassists to chance their arm were Oscar Pettiford and Nick Finton, while old and new drummers alike studied at the hands and feet of Klook. The list included Big Sid Catlett, Denzil Best, Doc West, Shadow Wilson and Taps Miller, and the group was often augmented by guitarist Charlie Christian.

Almost all had big band backgrounds but were intent not only on enjoying themselves at after-hours sessions but also on extending themselves instrumentally and broadening the scope of their musical outlooks. What their music actually sounded like at the time might easily have remained a mystery. Jazz students are

23

well aware of the myths and false legends that can build up if mere hearsay is trusted implicitly. At the turn of the century, New Orleans trumpeter legend Buddy Bolden was alternately described as an extremely loud musical incompetent and as a highly rhythmical player of great sensitivity.

Fortunately, the embryonic bebop movement had some documented evidence. Several people recorded the happenings at Minton's and Monroc's on primitive equipment. In most cases, the outcome was dire but, using his portable machine, enthusiast Jerry Newman managed to capture music that was good enough to issue on record. There is no evidence that anyone was paid a royalty, but at least posterity had its evidence.

If anything, it suggested that jazz was gradually evolving and not subject to a cataclysmic change. The 1941 *Stardust* was dominated by a rhapsodic tenor, either Don Byas, Chu Berry or both, who treated the melody with all the romantic overstatement of the swing era. Gillespie was similarly conservative, his note production was below par and, although his timing was suitably oblique, it was a performance decidedly less assured than the 1939 *Hot Mallets*.

In contrast, *Kerovac* was more ambitious, and it included the odd arpeggio drilled in a half-tone higher than the prevalent chord should have decreed. Gillespie was not in especially great lip, however, and a few notes were cracked as the more difficult intervals were essayed. The rhythmic emphasis remained loyal to the riff build-up of the swing tradition, but accents were laid differently. Regrettably, this more fragmented approach was not helped by a dull, metronomical drummer listed in most discographies as Kenny Clarke but surely not the redoubtable Klook.

Charlie Parker was not present, but the modernisation programme had begun in earnest, and it was the after hours sessions that were encouraging it.

For a newly married man, artistic fulfillment pays few bills, however, and Gillespie needed permanent employment. A brief spell with Ella Fitzgerald's band did not work out, and a spell at New York's Kelly's Stables, first with Coleman Hawkins and then with Benny Carter, promised rather more. Klook was in the Carter combo and, during a brief stay, Gillespie and the drummer introduced a wider club audience to what was becoming recognised as the new music.

The big bands still seemed to offer a feeling of security and permanence and, when in 1942 Gillespie had the opportunity to join the all white Charlie Barnet Orchestra for a tour, he accepted willingly. One of the added attractions that the trumpeter offered to any prospective employer was that he was not about to be

24

conscripted for the Army draft. He had declared himself a pacifist when approached in 1940 and, after putting his case rather forcibly, had been turned down for service.

This was just as well because, on 7 December 1941, the Japanese attacked Pearl Harbor and America was committed to war. The rate of service induction increased and a large number of musicians joined the forces. Gillespie's immunity made him an attractive property for a leader struggling to keep his band together, but, despite this, his association with Barnet did not last. Gillespie enjoyed the idea of a regular salary, the normal terms of employment in the white bands, but he found the music rather stylised and, after the tour, moved on to the band of Les Hite.

The Illinois born saxophonist and pianist had established a reputation on the West Coast. His early thirties band had included Lionel Hampton and he had backed Louis Armstrong on important records of the era. He had often used tours to New York as an opportunity to strengthen his band, and it was under such circumstances that he recruited Gillespie in 1942.

The Hite band already included another promising young trumpeter in Joe Wilder but Gillespie's reputation had gone before him. Hite wanted him but he did experience some trepidation; he had heard of the Calloway incident and was somewhat in awe of his new horn man. In the event, the forward looking Gillespie did not fit in. He did just enough to satisfy his leader and went so far as to actually record with him, but he could not come to terms with the rhythm section. A rift began and, after a clash with the band's drummer, the young trumpeter found himself the only player not 'rehired' when the orchestra was temporarily disbanded.

Almost at once he joined Lucky Millinder and, in so doing, put himself in the employment of another leader with an eccentric method of firing sidemen. Lucius Millinder was not really a musician himself but he was a superb showman as well as a skilled organizer. In the thirties, he had fronted the underrated Mills Blue Rhythm Band and began leading a group under his own name in 1940. His own band played the soundtrack for the 1940 film *Paradise in Harlem* and, during its life up to 1952, included such luminaries as altoist Tab Smith, tenor saxophonist Lucky Thompson, pianist Bill Doggett and the not inconsiderable guitar and vocal talent of Sister Rosetta Tharpe.

Despite his own lack of musical knowledge, Millinder did have a unique ear for musical arrangements. In a casual conversation taped in Canada, Gillespie described Lucky Millinder as 'the best conductor I ever had'. With typical flamboyance he went on to say that 'Lucky Millinder could conduct a band better than any one in the world, including Toscanini!'

He told of Chappie Willett, the band's arranger at that time, and a man who introduced strange time signatures – 'a lot of weird things like 3/8, 5/8, 12/8 and 16/95' (the last followed by a typical Gillespie chuckle). It transpired that 'Lucky Millinder would sit down and listen to Chappie taking rehearsals. After a couple of days Chappie would say – "O.K. Lucky, you got it".' From then on Millinder had it down and 'You would not have to count with Lucky. When it was time for you . . . you got seven bars out . . . on the fourth bar he's doing this to you with his finger – like the trumpet – you put your horn up at that point and, when his hand came down, you start reading and keep reading.'

During his brief stay with the band, Gillespie recorded only four tunes. On *Little John Special* his leader's hand certainly came down at the right moment because the young horn man fashioned two unpredictable blues choruses that monitored his continued growth in confidence. Millinder was obviously impressed but he was an eccentric leader and he seemed to take a savage delight in sacking people. Gillespie told how 'Lucky would fire anybody, Lucky fired himself one time. He'd fire you and, when he realised he still wanted you in his band, would hire you back and give you more money.'

The uncertainty unsettled Gillespie and, after being released for the nth time, refused the invitation to return. As a second string, he had been producing big band scores on a freelance basis. His earlier experience with Calloway had proved invaluable, and he had begun to regard arranging as a skill to place in parallel with his trumpet playing. Both Woody Herman and Jimmy Dorsey bought items from him, although the latter, in particular, had problems with the phrase shapes, as Gillespie began to introduce a new brand of timing and cadence into his charts.

Nevertheless, his real interest was in playing, and he actually returned to Philadelphia late in 1942 to lead his own group at the Down Beat Club. It was, in some ways a move of convenience; he could live with his mother and could suit himsef as regards his coming and going. Musically, he was now regarded as something of a star, and he was able to inculcate the ways of his modern music into the local players. It was hardly a demanding situation but it had its distinct consolations in terms of freedom from stress.

It was a short lived respite from the turmoil of big bands, however, and when Earl Hines came to town with a band interested in the new music, Gillespie joined. The clincher was the news that Charlie Parker was also about to join the band, but what the trumpeter did not know was that 'Bird' had been persuaded to enlist by being told that Gillespie was already signed, sealed and collected.

Whatever the reasons for the move, it was one that worked out well. In addition to Parker, the band included the talents of trumpeter Benny Harris, trombonist Bennie Green, saxophonist Scoops Carry, drummer Shadow Wilson and vocalists Billy Eckstine and Sarah Vaughan. As with all Earl Hines bands, the music was dominated by its pianist leader. This was not something that disappointed his sidemen and, in fact, they often encouraged him to extend his solo interludes. Hines usually responded in his superbly professional way and Gillespie has often acknowledged how much he derived from the pianist in terms of self-discipline and organization.

More important, his presence in the band gave Gillespie the chance to examine the music of other forward looking players and to test his own ideas against them. These men were his peers and this made the quest the more challenging. No one was more challenging than Parker, and the men began their unique musical relationship as much off stage as on. They practised back-stage and in hotel rooms and each offered important theoretical inputs into the music of the other.

With genuine candour, Gillespie said, 'I think I was a little more advanced, harmonically, than he was. But, rhythmically, he was quite advanced with setting up the phrase and how you get from one note to another . . . Charlie Parker heard rhythms and rhythmic patterns differently and after we started playing together, I began to play rhythmically, more like him.'

This perhaps implies that Gillespie was the schooled player and that Parker was the intuitive one. It is a theory that has gained credence in some critical circles but is a dangerous, over-simplification. An examination of their origins, their individual paths of musical self discovery and the nature of their fully formulated style denies such an assumption. If it was the trumpeter who brought to the new music a greater harmonic insight and the altoist (actually a tenor in the Hines band) who showed the more intense, rhythmic emphasis, it was only a matter of degree. No useful purpose is to be served by evaluating either man in respect of his contribution.

Certainly, the Hines band fostered their musical interaction, and it was unfortunate that Gillespie quit to join a Billy Eckstine band that never happened. It was a step that again left him without a job, but he was by then a well-known player. So much so that he was invited to 'dep' in the Duke Ellington band for just over one month toward the end of 1943.

It could have been the answer to a dream, a chance to join the music's greatest jazz orchestra. Unfortunately, as has happened in the past, induction into the band was not a simple matter. The band's lack of organisation, the leader's own irresponsible assumption that any new sideman would know his 'book' and the at times open hostility of certain sidemen, were daunting factors.

They certainly deterred Gillespie, and he was more than happy that he was not offered a permanent post.

From the point of view of both parties, it must be seen as an artistic opportunity lost. Ellington's unique talent for introducing ostensibly alien talents into his established line-up and for making the fusion work were well known. Gillespie's embryonic, bebop style of 1943 could have been quite a stimulant, especially when one considers how successfully Ellington used similarly motivated players, such as Clark Terry and Willie Cook, for much of the fifties.

Gillespie did actually record for the band, albeit on V-discs, the only legitimate recordings allowed during the union ban operating at that time. Later a whole session appeared on World Transcriptions but, even by the time that the V-discs appeared, the trumpeter had moved on.

Back again in the employment marketplace of New York, he worked briefly with the John Kirby Sextet. This was a strange choice for both employer and employee. Kirby was a subtle bassist with a light touch, and his 'Biggest Little Band in the Land' was distinguished by its understated rhythm section and by the superbly wrought and softly textured unisons of its three-horn

Billy Eckstine

28

Outside Birdland

front line. It had established a reputation for gently jazzing such 'classics' as Grieg's *Anitra's Dance* Dvořák's *Humoresque*, Tchaikovsky's *Sugar Plum Fairy* and Donizetti's *Sextet from Lucia di Lammermoor* and it literally personified conservative good taste.

Gillespie did not officially record with the Kirby band, but a radio transcription from May 1944 was later issued with him in the group alongside Buster Bailey and Ben Webster. The results were pleasing but this was no place for an adventurous trumpeter who was bursting to give his new musical ideas to the world.

More suitable was a project in which he became involved a month later. Billy Eckstine's band-that-never-was finally took off. Band booker Billy Shaw had tried to persuade the singer to front a band from St. Louis led by George Hudson. Gillespie and saxophonist Budd Johnson were on hand at the time and, no doubt

Sarah Vaughan

out of vested interest, pointed out that, at the end of the proposed tour, most of the musicians would want to return home. Better, they argued, to build up the personnel on a more permanent basis, so that a return to New York would find the band still intact.

Eckstine was won over; he made Gillespie his musical director, and together they set about recruiting a band. Many of the men who had left Earl Hines with Eckstine were still available and a very good line-up was rapidly assembled. In the spring of 1944, the band, featuring Charlie Parker and Sarah Vaughan, opened in Wilmington, Delaware. On the night of the opening, they were armed with only two specialist charts, one of which was Gillespie's *Night in Tunisia*. This meant that they had to use stock arrangements for the more commercial items, but this was not a situation that restricted the band's inherently progressive attitude. The trumpeter has always maintained that it was a bebop band from the word 'go', and Eckstine has since substantiated that view.

With a line-up that was later to include saxophonists Gene Ammons, Dexter Gordon, Sonny Stitt and Wardell Gray, as well as trumpeters Fats Navarro, Miles Davis and Howard McGhee, there really was little doubt. Gillespie later began to provide quite a few arrangements, as did Budd Johnson, Tadd Dameron and Jerry Valentine, and the music was a unique hybrid, falling somewhere between the later hothouse bebop and the more forward looking swing bands of the forties.

Fortunately, the presence of so many all-star soloists did not affect the discipline in the band's ensemble passages. The five-man reed section fed bebop into the orchestral bloodstream, they flowed like a single saxophonist and they prepared the ear for the solo features that were such an important part of the Eckstine oeuvre.

The trumpet section sometimes included the leader himself and, as a unit, they pumped fire into the most staid material. Only the rhythm section failed to respond to the ideas of the new music. Neither bassist Tommy Potter nor drummer Art Blakey had, at this stage, mastered the diffused rhythmic accentuation demanded by the music. Both later became giants of bop but, in 1944/5, they avoided what they did not know and provided what can best be described as orthodox big-band patterns.

Sonny Stitt

Tadd Dameron

Bearing this in mind, it is perhaps surprising that the band did not get much public acclaim. Stories abound of bookers, club owners and members of the audience complaining that they could not dance to the music. The band featured stunning bop solos by Parker, Gillespie and Navarro, but airshots from 1945 attest to the fact that Potter and Blakey conspired to give the band a strong 'foot-tapping' quality. Listening to an item like *Airmail Special*, it is difficult to imagine how anyone could accuse them of failing to stir the dancers into action.

The criticism was there, however, and, because of it, the band had a hard time. Frequently younger audiences stood and listened to the brilliant soloists – but people rarely danced for long. Dance halls in the Middle West, in particular, knew what they wanted and, in their book, they did not get it with the Eckstine band.

The comparative lack of commercial acceptance did not affect the band's musical aspirations, and Gillespie was a major influence on its policy. In particular, he coached trumpeters in the new ways but, more significantly, encouraged each of the 'sections' to phrase straight passages with the off centre accents of bop.

Gillespie has often commented that the music of that era reflected its historical situation. World War II was coming to a dreadful and violent climax, and yet many of the old values remained. Bebop took in both shades of opinion, and a band like Eckstine's, for all its aesthetic value, failed because it did not fully satisfy either. The serviceman on leave, perhaps dreading the personal danger to himself that the war presented, associated with the sentimentality of the leader's own vocals and certainly would have enjoyed the contributions of band guests like Lena Horne.

His indifference to the experimental wing of the band was understandable. At home the serviceman was with people he knew and, like them, he wanted the security of tradition. Enough of the unknown awaited him in Europe or on the Pacific Islands south of Japan, without the challenge of 'new' music at base. Eckstine perhaps felt this more than did his sidemen, and much emphasis was placed on his commercial vocals. In retrospect, one must say that he struck a reasonable compromise, using most of his recording studio opportunities to present the voice but reserving certain items as showcases for his band.

In this respect, Eckstine was not well served by his recordings, made mainly for National. They were badly balanced and generally poorly produced and it was, in many ways, like history repeating itself. In the late twenties and thirties, the all-star Fletcher Henderson Orchestra had been a band revered by its contemporaries. Its records, however, had rarely done justice to the superb musicians involved and the band had been damned with faint praise. The Eckstine situation was similar and the reports of those who heard this exciting band get little support from recorded evidence.

Gillespie's own praise for them was considerable and, in view of his down-to-earth criticism of bands he felt were below the highest standards, must be taken seriously. He left Eckstine only because he wanted to stay in New York and because he was ready to enter a more specialized musical arena.

CHAPTER 3

52nd STREET THEME

After leaving Eckstine in 1944, Gillespie settled, at least musically, in 'The Street'. A thoroughfare that provided a home for a very important slice of jazz history, 52nd Street was situated in the block between New York's 5th and 6th Avenues. Things have changed a great deal since then, but (in 1944) it underwent a cultural and visual metamorphosis every day at dusk. By day it was a seedy collection of rag trade warehouses, export confirming houses, homes for language and music teachers, struggling graphics companies and the offices of private eyes. As daylight finally surrendered to the shadows of the huge surrounding buildings, a transformation took place.

As the artisans of the day deserted their posts, the night brought its own garish magic. Squalor hid behind flashing neon signs, the walls sprouted club entrances and they pushed out their protective awnings to usher patrons from car to door. These canopies varied as much in age and colour as did the clubs, but the list of performers who walked up their aisles and through the doors was something of a Who's Who of jazz.

In Jimmy Ryan's, at the time, the music might have been built around the Bixian sound of Jimmy McPartland's cornet or the throbbing insistence of Sidney Bechet's soprano saxophone. The Onyx Club often boasted the presence of the proudly elegant Coleman Hawkins with some of the young lions of the new music, while at the Famous Door pianists flocked to worship the flawless skills of Art Tatum. Fats Waller had often brought his multifarious skills to the Spotlight, but the catalogue of attraction was endless.

Non musical activities swung on both sides of the law and, although shady dealing meant ownership of the clubs changed constantly, the mood amongst most of the players was ebullient. Whether playing in the major groups or appearing in the supporting bands, most musicians felt it was a privilege to be

Max Roach

working with their peers. For many it was a relief from arduous touring with the big bands, the wages were at least acceptable and the challenge of the combo situation was an added artistic attraction.

Gillespie joined bassist Oscar Pettiford at the Onyx in a group that intially included pianist George Wallington and drummer Max Roach. The leader, born on an Indian reservation at Okmulgee, Oklahoma, in 1922, had been a regular habitué at Minton's, and his highly sophisticated style traced a logical line from the earlier inspirations of Duke Ellingtons's Jimmy Blanton. His reaction to the needs of bebop were instinctive and with Roach he formed a formidable, rhythmic duo. Wallington's piano line was almost a thing apart, but the pair were helped by his unobtrusive attitudes.

Here was a pianist who sensed when he might be needed with directional chords, but he also knew when to 'lay out'.

Gillespie and Pettiford had, not suprisingly, wanted Charlie Parker as a member of the group but, in a mix up in correspondence, the Bird failed to make it. His replacement was Don Byas, another Oklahoman and a tenor saxophonist with extensive experience in the big bands of the thirties. Through his involvement with the Mintonian experiments, Byas had progressed beyond this stylistic area, however, and had added his big, luxurious tone to the rhythmic and harmonic deviations of bop.

The group rapidly developed into a cohesive unit; they frequently did not bother with naming the tunes they played, but Gillespie has told the interesting story about the derivation of the media's use of the word bop. The trumpeter would often use an onomatopoeic scat phrase to remind his fellows of a particular melody line. Perhaps because of its natural finality, these expressions often ended with the sound 'bop' and audiences were quick to pick up on the fact. They began to use the term in requesting themes they liked, and visiting journalists had themselves a ready-made buzz word.

Gillespie has always maintained that the term bebop first appeared in the American press during his Onyx residency, and his tune *Bebop* was certainly written at that time. Nevertheless, it was not only music that distinguished the happenings at the Onyx. Gillespie and his colleagues had begun to attract a cult following of some magnitude. The trumpeter's appearance was taken as a model, and sartorial compliance came to be taken as an important part of the bop ethic. Fans took to wearing similar berets, sporting heavy, horn-rimmed glasses and, if possible, growing goatee beards.

A language grew up to support the movement's exclusivity. It sought to create a mood of relaxed unflappability, and to be 'cool' was to have mastered the mysteries of the music. Once you had, you became 'hip', a variation on the previous generation's 'hep' and proof that your attitude was modern.

Bop had become the music of 'The Street' and it was almost inevitable that Gillespie should share his talents around other clubs. He played in the Downbeat with tenor saxophonist Budd Johnson, pianist Clyde Hart, bassist Leonard Gaskin and with Max Roach again on drums. As a group, its grasp of bop was less convincing but, with Gillespie and Roach sharing the driving seat, the band negotiated the new music's difficulties without too many obvious clashes.

Gillespie even strayed outside the confines of The Street, and at Kelly's Stables in Greenwich Village he took part in modern jam sessions. These developed much as had those at Minton's and Monroe's, except that they were not 'after hours' events and, in fact, shattered the serenity of Sunday afternoons. Gillespie's contribution was tremendous and he became proselytizer as much as player, with young players coming to drink at the didactic fountain in large numbers.

The New York jazz scene had really come to life with the sounds of bop. Giants of the past like Coleman Hawkins were steeping themselves in the new traditions while reactionary critics sought to justify their inability to grasp the music's true implications. The jazz public had no such problems and Gillespie was quick to grasp the commercial implications of what was happening.

On the strength of this, he decided to form a big band, perhaps along the lines of the Eckstine unit but with an even more uncompromisingly boppish direction. In some ways, this was made easier by the fact that his former leader was losing interest in having a modern jazz orchestra. Gillespie took several of his best sidemen and Eckstine raised no serious objections.

The big band undertook a tour of the South. The year was 1945 and the members of the band shared their leader's conviction that they could sell their music to the black audiences on the tour. In fact, they had totally misjudged the situation. The South's taste for the blues remained steadfast, the crowds wanted to dance and there was no provision in the itinerary for seated concerts.

Gillespie was desolated. The South was not about to be wooed by the auxiliary attractions of the touring party. The fleet footed dancing of the Nicholas Brothers, the comedy of Patterson and Jackson, the singing of June Eckstine and various novelty chorus girl acts held little appeal and the music offered no old-time blues. The trumpeter returned to New York and immediately disbanded.

In the meantime his soul brother Parker had been far from inactive. After leaving Eckstine, he had been invited to play at the Three Deuces on The Street. The house trio at the time included pianist Joe Albany, bassist Curly Russell and drummer Stan Levey, but after accepting the job Parker agitated for the hiring of another horn player. His choice was inevitably Gillespie, but at first the trumpeter would not say yes to proprietor Sammy Kaye.

Finally, agreement was reached and, with Al Haig replacing Albany, the quintet line-up was set. Here was the bare bones of bebop. Russell's pulse was basic and had not moved too far from the regular 4/4 pulse of his big band experience with Don Redman and Benny Carter. Haig, however, had learned from Bud Powell; he had similarly adapted the phrase shapes of Gillespie and Parker to the needs of the piano, and his delivery was a reminder that the piano was a percussion instrument. Levey had as assiduously observed the Klook method and his urgent, cross rhythms emphasized the loosely moving backgrounds that the horns found conducive to their needs.

This rhythmic element was very important to Gillespie, and it is instructive to examine other less successful rhythm sections with which he worked at the time. With young drummer Shelly Manne he made two sessions, one including the little-known bassist Murray Shipinski and the other with Pettiford. With the Oklahoman he was more at home, although it was immediately evident that it was the bass line that provided the calibration amidst Manne's rather confused figures on the ride cymbal.

Cozy Cole got no such assistance from Slam Stewart on a later session. As befitted a man who had made his recording debut with Jelly Roll Morton in 1930, Cole chonked along with his swing era shuffle, mercifully unobrusive, dove-tailing with the similarly inappropriate bass but offering no inspirational input.

Gillespie fared no better in groups led by others. In Red Norvo's Selected Sextet, drummer J. C. Heard sounded happier with brushes behind pianist Teddy Wilson than he did with his stick work in support of Gillespie, Parker and Flip Phillips. Even worse was Clyde Hart's All Stars, with the leader's piano nondescript and bassist Al Hall and drummer 'Specs' Powell projecting in a distinctly dated manner.

Only Big Sid Catlett of the 'wrong' drummers made any worthwhile contribution and this he did, not trying to use the new style, but by deliberately avoiding it. He was certainly more versatile than any of the percussionists listed above and he made his impact by asserting his own personality within the new ethic. He played with natural relaxation with both Parker and Gillespie and, most especially, behind Sarah Vaughan on the May Guild label session. He made no attempt at 'bomb dropping' in the bebop manner but did punctuate with immense authority.

Good though Haig, Russell and Levey were, it was the principals that created the bop quintet formula. The difficult unisons were easily available to their techniques because they thought and phrased alike. The flatted fifth became their 'blue note' and it characterized their style. The harmonic base of their music became a framework, and the flowing, multi-noted runs that filled them out could take any related, melodic route. The astute Joachim Berendt once likened bop to 'musical shorthand', and in the harmonic sense he was totally right. What that theory overlooked was the considerable amount of musical rhethoric that the shorthand or harmonic frame was asked to carry.

The important point was that, with the quintet, the transition from melodic to harmonically based jazz was complete. The language of bop gradually moved into every fabric of music, not only jazz but into almost every dance band in the 'Western' world.

Dizzy in front of a poster of Charlie Parker

This was to remain the case up to the time of the free form revolution in the late fifties and until the strong influence of rhythm and blues was felt in popular music shortly after.

Working with Parker was easy for Gillespie. They liked each other and, in the turmoil of life in The Street, 'looked out' for each other. Both were intelligent men but it was the altoist who paraded the fact. Whereas Gillespie was the up-front, on-stage extrovert, it was Parker who would seek out the after hours discussion, to look for a chance to flex his intellectual muscles in public.

He was also more susceptible to the sycophants and this led him into bad company. It seems probable that Parker had already become involved with drug use while still at school but, by becoming involved with the twilight world at the fringe of jazz, he denied himself any chance of avoiding hopeless addiction.

In contrast, Gillespie avoided this group of 'friends' as much as was practical. He had a wife to return to after a gig and, in any case, was not enamoured of many of the Bird's associates. Amazingly, he never saw his close colleague using drugs but he was very aware of the consequences. Many was the time he would remonstrate with Parker for using 'shit' (heroin) but only because of the spaced-out state in which Parker managed to get himself. Parker usually treated his guardian to sympathy or amazed indifference and Gillespie liked him too much to make it an incontravertable issue.

Sadly, Parker's affliction was to adversely affect the next stage of Gillespie's career. He had been offered a gig at Billy Berg's in Hollywood, California. The contract was for eight weeks and was for a quintet. The idea appealed to Gillespie and, although he had no hesitation in hiring Parker, he took the precaution of engaging vibraphonist Milt Jackson just in case anybody became indisposed. In principle, Gillespie enjoyed the trip but he tended to gloss over the problems that could be caused by taking a fully committed heroin addict to a place where there could be a supply problem.

In fact, troubles even occurred on the train journey to the West Coast. Ross Russell described in *Bird Lives!* how the altoist broke train on route in search of a fix. Finally, he had to be strapped into his bunk and, by the time he arrived in California, he was in a very bad state. Fortunately, a reliable supply was found and, although he missed the first set on the opening night, he made the final one to turn the group's West Coast debut into a major triumph.

Musically, this tended to be the case during their entire stay. Ray Brown had taken over Russell's bass chair and this was a further improvement to the group. Jackson was on hand when Parker failed to make it but the altoist had more good than bad moments. It almost amounted to the fact that, if he had a good 'score', he would play superbly. If he did not, he might not appear at all.

Another problem was the proprietor, Billy Berg. He had no interest in modern jazz, did not know what bebop was and had probably been badly advised in booking the band. For their part, the band enjoyed the sunshine, delighted that large numbers of local musicians flocked to hear them and showed absolutely no inclination to compromise their programme. Unfortunately, after the initial enthusiasm, the musicians began to stop by less frequently, the novelty wore off amongst local followers and the once packed crowd began to show threadbare traces.

Berg was interested only in commercial viability. Estranged members of the less-hip audiences began to ask for the band to sing or to play straight ballads and the situation at the club began to sour. It finally got to the stage at which Gillespie was glad to play out his time and get back to the more enlightened crowds in New York. In the last week, Parker went missing completely and Gillespie, torn between loyalty to his friend and complete exasperation at the situation, was finally reduced to leaving his salary and transportation money at the hotel in the hope that he would claim it.

History has since recorded that the hapless Parker ended up drying out in Camarillo State Hospital and, in a strange way, this seemed to bring down the final curtain on a tour that started in triumph and ended in disaster. Even the one record session that Parker and Gillespie made while on tour was strange.

Alternating with them at Berg's had been Slim Gaillard, the notorious forties 'hipster'. His group included the talented Dodo Marmarosa on piano, but things between the Vout Orenee man and Gillespie were never particularly good. Nevertheless, a recording date had been set up and Gaillard featured in his zany, vocal style. From Gillespie's point of view, the use of the nonchalant, New Orleans bounce of Zutty Singleton's drums rather than his own team was not a formula for success, and so it proved. Gaillard mugged his way through a comedy vocal on *Slim's Jam*, which was at least an amusing opus, but neither Parker nor Gillespie played with much sense of involvement.

CHAPTER 4

GROOVIN' HIGH

Gillespie's return to New York in 1946 inevitably meant returning to The Street. It also gave him the chance to have a troublesome lip fixed and to be in good shape for the renewal of his battle with the establishment. In many ways the victory was almost his already; bop had certainly won over the city's more musically aware public and Gillespie had become a popular figure. In fact, on his return, he found that the Three Deuces and the Spotlite were vying for his services.

Faced with this very acceptable dilemma, he chose the Spotlite. It was owned by his old associate from the Uptown House, Clark Monroe. It was a larger room and he was promised that, should his smaller group prove successful there, he could introduce his own big band. This latter point was the obvious clincher and with the brilliant twenty-two-year-old Sonny Stitt replacing Parker, he opened at the club.

All went well, Monroe was as good as his word and Gillespie set about forming his orchestra. Billy Shaw agreed to arrange bookings away from the club and also other business, but the trumpeter himself was determined that this time he would keep the band together. The bitter experience of the previous year had taught him many things and it was obvious that he could not do everything himself.

Fortunately, he recruited composer and arranger Walter (Gil) Fuller to assemble and direct the band. Fuller was a Californian but he had trained in New York. He had considerbale experience with the big-band situation and had written for Les Hite, Floyd Ray, Jimmy Lunceford and Tiny Bradshaw. Gillespie had got to know him while he had been writing for Eckstine and was satisfied that his knowledge of the bop idiom and his unquestionable organisational talent made him an ideal choice.

The accommodating Eckstine was again invited to assist. He

allowed arrangements to be copied and also stumped up with microphones, equipment and uniforms. There had not been much time to get the band organised but, for once in his life, Gillespie found the sea calm and the winds steady.

Monroe himself was equally excited and put up a huge banner with the legend 'Dizzy Gillespie's Big Band' emblazoned across it. With journalistic excess it might have been said that the opening night 'stopped The Street', but there was no doubt that it did make an impact.

Choosing the personnel had not been easy. Despite the pioneer work by Eckstine and by Gillespie's own first big-band, there was no established vernacular for bebop in the big band context. It still threatened to be something of a hydbrid, taking its inspiration from bop and using the tricks of group momentum from the swing era. Recruitment tended to be divided between those who could provide inspirational solos and those whose credentials included proven, group capabilities.

Howard Johnson was chosen to lead the reed section. The altoist had been with Gillespie on the Teddy Hill 1937 tour of Europe but he had experience that stretched back to the bands of Charlie Johnson, Chick Webb and the master of reed voicings, Benny Carter. Baritone saxophonist Cecil Payne became the sheet anchor of that section and stamped his superbly throaty authority on the reeds until the early months of 1949.

Dave Burns became a stalwart of the trumpet section. A former Dizzy fan, he remained in the band for three years. Trumpeters such as Miles Davis, Kinney Dorham and Freddie Webster all had spells with the band and Willie Cook later came in to add his own individual sparkle.

Initially, Max Roach and Kenny Clarke occupied the drum stool, and first Thelonious Monk and then John Lewis did the keyboard duties. Charles Greenlee and Bill Shepherd were amongst the prominent trombonists used but, finally, it was Fuller's writing that gave the band its highly idiosyncratic personality. The reeds, in particular, were nurtured, and Fuller explained just how he achieved such a unique sound. 'We let nobody in there use vibrato, except the first man, so that when the saxophonist played, they had a distinctive sound . . . I used all open harmony for the saxophones all the way through, then close harmony for the trumpets, and spread out three trombones. That's what gave the brass that big, fat sound . . . Not even Dizzy knew what the hell I was doing.'

This was, no doubt, a rather sweeping statement. If there was one thing that Gillespie did know it was the brass sound that he wanted. The trumpets phrased as one man and that one man was Gillespie! It could never have been enough, merely to write out parts; the trumpets had to capture the cadence, the tone and even the unerring confidence of the leader, in order to reproduce his solo voice in unison.

The trumpets certainly traded in excitement; the emphasis was on high register areas and, whatever the tempo, they produced a genuine thrust. Thanks to Fuller, the reeds achieved a similar urgency; not for them the sighing romanticism of the swing era but rather a latent combustability, a smouldering element ready to ignite at any given moment.

In view of the band's forward-looking attitude, it was perhaps surprising that single instruments from one section were not integrated into others. The pattern of the band remained one of section interplay in the traditional manner, almost the call-and-response of the primitive big bands. The end result, however, suggested no such backward attitude; even in its rougher moments, the band demanded attention and, as trumpets competed with reeds, bebop remained the common language.

Almost as an extraneous extra, the band enjoyed the mercurial skills of vibraphonist Milt Jackson. His brittle but articulate solos came as a thing apart, almost as if he had assumed the role of musical observer in the main battle between trumpets and saxophones. Singer Alice Roberts, provided no such service and her archly cool singing seemed very much at odds with the authenticity of the band.

Nevertheless, singing did play an important part in the band's growing popularity. It was becoming commercially successful and was gaining unqualified acceptance in places that had initially been very reserved. It would have been pleasing to report that this success was based purely on its quality and on the skill of its soloists. Unfortunately, this was not entirely the case. The eccentricity of dress, the deliberate exploitation of bebop's giddiness and, most particularly, the use of the leader's consciously frivolous singing were major factors in selling the band to the public.

As a policy it certainly worked and, by 1947, Gillespie's was the band to follow, whether you be musician or fan. This, however, overlooked one very significant fact. For all its enforced idiocy and visual gesture, Gillespie's singing style, with its emphasis on wordless scat, changed the rules of the jazz vocal for the first time since Armstrong sang with Fletcher Henderson in 1924.

As with Armstrong's, the quality of the voice was, by normal standards, dismal. One could hardly talk in terms of range, yet Gillespie organised his wordless gibberish with a draughtsman's hand. Inevitably, he phrased his phonetic shorthand in the same style as his trumpet, although it must be said that the limitations in his voice reduced his options. He could not fall back on the masterful technique of his horn and he could not 'showboat' into the upper register.

He was a prisoner within the confines of an extraordinarily limited vocal situation and he had no alternative but to extricate himself from melodic cul-de-sacs by sleight of voice creativity. To do so he demonstrated amazing dexterity, disguising the limited number of sounds he used by the shaping of the solo and by the unpredictable direction of his melodic line. Much had been made of Miles Davis's use of his limitations – Gillespie's vocals added a new dimension to that premise.

Dizzy with Joe Williams (left) and Jon Henricks

45

The Gillespie 'pouches'

As important as they were, such oral gymnastics were only part of the band's armaments. Fortunately, their perpetrator was not unaware of their worth and he exploited them as part of his campaign to gain recognition for his orchestra. In fact, he was almost on the brink of a break-through. The red-letter day occurred in September 1947, when the Gillespie Band played at Carnegie Hall with Ella Fitzgerald. At the time, this was still the jazzman's ultimate accolade and, when the date was suggested by Billy Shaw, Gillespie was somewhat concerned. In the event, his worries were more than a little misplaced. The concert was something of a triumph; the leader played superbly and important American media organs acknowledged the fact. It seemed almost from that moment the band began to win over the swing era reactionaries and take its position alongside Duke Ellington, Count Basie and Woody Herman.

It was also at this time that the first was seen of what later became known medically as Gillespie's Pouches. As he began playing, his cheeks would swell in a most peculiar manner. He

46

experienced no pain and, in fact, was very much at ease with this state of affairs. It required added control, but it suited him and he remained loyal to the frog-like appearance from that period onward.

More important the band's improved status at last began to bring some degree of financial security. In earlier times the erratic attendance record of Parker and Monk had been tolerated because of the tunes they brought to the 'book'. Had more money been available they might well have been retained as writers only, but in the circumstances they were finally dismissed.

Gillespie particularly regretted the departure of the prodigious and gifted Monk. He was on a high compositional curve and his material would have been invaluable to the band. Finally, his transgressions became impossible and he left to make way for John

Thelonious Monk

Lewis, a less inspired pianist and composer but a far more reliable human being. In his defence, it must be said that Lewis was at least a forward-looking writer and, together with the young and highly talented George Russell, he made a valuable addition to the team of Fuller and the leader.

Ironically, it was the arrival of a far more intuitive talent that was to revolutionize the band's music during 1947. It also greatly affected Gillespie's musical attitudes and resurrected thoughts he had had regarding musical fusions while still with the Cab Calloway Band. It was then that Gillespie had become interested in Cuban music and had discussed it with Mario Bauza, a colleague in Calloway's trumpet section. Bauza had been born in Havana and had come to America in 1931. He felt that there were possibilities of such a fusion and, on hearing of his old friend's renewed interest, recommended that he should hear Chano Pozo, a fellow-countryman living in New York.

Luciano Pozo y Gonzales was born in Cuba in 1915 and from an early age had become interested in West African music. Through this interest, he had developed remarkable skills as a percussionist, dancer and composer, although his specialities were the bongo and conga drums. During his early twenties, he had become strongly associated with a strange Nigerian sect, the Abakwa, and through them had made his name in the island's Mardi Gras events.

His meeting with Gillespie was not easy. He spoke no English but was, to some extent, won over by the trumpeter's friendly, outgoing manner. In any event, he agreed to join the band and to take his place in a rhythm section whose playing must have seemed an immeasurable distance from his own rhythmic aspirations. His solution was simple. He divided his induction period between teach-in and learn-in; taking basic, rhythmic instructions from Gillespie and teaching his fellows in the rhythm team the mysteries of African cross-rhythms.

His effect on the band was joyously subversive and he made an inestimable contribution to the creation of the brilliantly exciting music that became known as 'cubop'. Afro-Cuban jazz had arrived; the band's reeds took on an almost Carribbean swirl; the brass continued to shout its 52nd Street message while Pozo scuttled above, below and through the ensemble.

As might be expected, it was drummer Max Roach and bassist Al McKibbon who experienced the greatest problems, but Pozo taught them by relating all aspects of rhythmic interaction to the drum. He also involved Gillespie and there is no doubt that the trumpeter's ability as a percussionist stems from this period. Pozo's skills as a teacher must certainly have been exceptional because very soon, the large rhythm section had mastered the art of staying out of each other's way.

Photo: Mephisto

Dizzy Gillespie with Charles Delaunay, Paris 1952

The principals co-wrote *Manteca*, and Russell's two-part *Cubana Be, Cubana Bop* became the anthem to the style. Even more than before, the band generated immense excitement; lyrical moments were imbued with tension by the busy muttering of Pozo's percussion figures, while his chanting added an ethnic reality to the proceedings. In concert, only certain numbers were singled out for the pure Afro-Cuban treatment, but a huge extra dimension had been added to Gillespie's music.

Early in 1948, Pozo was part of the touring party when Gillespie took his now internationally known orchestra to Scandinavia. It would be tempting to describe the venture in the terms of the musical comedian who sees a situation as starting badly – and deteriorating! In real terms, it did get better but a bad start did put a blight on the trip.

The band was led to believe that they would be travelling in the *SS Drottningholm*'s first-class berths. They found themselves in tourist class on a trip that suffered from the North Sea at its most violent, and they arrived in Sweden three days late. There were mix-ups over accommodation but at least the band was well received. They toured extensively in Sweden and enjoyed similar success in Denmark. Unfortunately, the local promoter absconded with the players' money and they were, to all intents and purposes, stranded penniless and more than three thousand miles from home.

Gillespie and his men were nothing if not resourceful. An offer from the Hot Club de Belgique was taken up, an advance on salary

49

established and the band packed its bags for mainland Europe. In many ways this was uncharted territory, almost like starting again from scratch. The European jazz scene in 1948 was strangely insular, and it was inevitable that word of the band's Scandinavian triumphs had reached few Belgian ears. Despite this, the concerts were reasonably successful and at least the tour was back on an even keel.

The band's next patron was French critic and musicologist Charles Delaunay, a pioneer in discographical studies and the producer of the first serious discography, *The New Hot Discography* (Criterion), in that very year, 1948. He had become enamoured of the new music by way of records; he held Gillespie in high esteem and had, in fact, broken a lifetime friendship with colleague Hughes Panassié, when his fellow-critic had adopted a reactionary musical stance.

Delauney was thrilled to be able to help and he organised the band's move to Paris. For Gillespie, at least, it was a return to a city with fond memories, but he had hardly considered the change in circumstances since his visit with Teddy Hill. Paris was, as always, a city with no time for half-measures; its volatile audiences were as liable to bury a new musical style as they were to give it their unreserved approbation.

The Hill band had used a tried and trusted formula, and cabaret-orientated Parisians had got what they expected. The new arrivals were on far more shakey ground, few Frenchmen knew of bebop and, in any case, French jazz audiences in 1948 tended to be younger and more vociferous. In retrospect, this was probably the band's salvation. They played at the Salle Pleyel, the Champs Élysées Club and Les Ambassadeurs, and all three venues enjoyed full houses. Despite playing one entire concert without their sheet music, the band generated tremendous fire, and reports were that audience response was tremendous. Paris took bebop to its heart, and Gillespie had again walked the tightrope between triumph and disaster with a skill given only to the natural vaudevillian.

Concerts were also undertaken in Lyons and Marseilles, and further offers came in to tour Britain, Italy, Spain and Switzerland. British interest was stymied by its own musicians' union who were, at that time, vetoing all contracts for foreign musicians. This was regrettable but, even had circumstances been different, it is likely Gillespie would have declined. The tour had run its course and many of the sidemen were ready to return home.

CHAPTER 5

OOP-POP-A-DAH

Back in the United States, the bebop bandwagon rolled on. Gillespie's friend and brilliant drummer Kenny Clarke had remained in Europe but, with Nelson Boyd filling that vacancy, the band again essayed the West Coast. This time the tour was mainly a success. It opened at the Cricket Club in Los Angeles, played to vast crowds in a Long Beach concert and, finally, returned to Hollywood and Billy Berg's.

The bebop cult had reached epidemic proportions. the dressing up that had occurred at the Onyx had seemed like a harmless diversion, but in California it became almost self-parody. Opportunists began to sell complete uniforms for the aspiring bop fan – berets, 'bop glasses' and even comic, spotted ties that were dubbed 'bop bow ties'. More and more followers grew goatees, and some women even painted on grotesque facsimiles.

Well-known Hollywood celebrities became involved and being seen at Gillespie performances became a social necessity. It got to be that people were coming to watch people watching the band. Even famous starlets joined in the painted-goatee fetish and above it all Gillespie was the presiding guru, the authority on all matters pertaining to the bebop religion.

It must be said that Gillespie enjoyed the situation at the time. It appealed to his natural sense of humour and, without doubt, pushed the bop cause. In retrospect, it can be seen as a mixed blessing. It fitted the hedonistic attitudes of 1948 California, it was perhaps a dry run for the flower generation of the sixties, and it did provide magazine writers with some colourful copy. Unfortunately, the only thing in which the media seemed less interested was the music.

This was particularly unfortunate because the West Coast residency represented the high spot in the career of Gillespie's second band. The new rhythm section, still with Pozo dominant, had settled in quickly and the odd changes in personnel had had little effect on the players' collective performance. In fact, the grafting-in of altoist Ernie Henry and tenor saxophinist James Moody strengthened the available solo roster.

So it was to prove at a concert at Pasadena Civic Auditorium in July 1948. The scene had been set by the authorities, who encouraged all supporters dressed in Dizzy-bop regalia to sit on or at the side of the stage. It was a situation ready made for a little theatre, and Gillespie was primed to exploit it. He mugged, he danced and generally played to the crowd. His mood was infectious and both band and audience took off. Some have likened the concert to Duke Ellington's dramatic 1956 Newport Festival, with its stunning *Diminuendo and Crescendo in Blue* but, whatever the comparison, it represented the band's artistic apex of the year.

Fortunately, the events were recorded and later issued on promoter Gene Norman's own record label. The bonus was that the recording captured the atmosphere of the concert as well as the precise musical happenings, thereby allowing later observers a look at the band at its best as well as possibly a band at the brink of dissolution. Musically, it was superb. Pozo buzzed dramaticaly, the brass shrieked their protest and the reeds swung remorselessly. Henry spoke eloquently on *Round About Midnight*, Moody offered his special brand of loquacious logic to *Ool-Ya-Koo*, while the leader dominated almost every title.

Gillespie was his best on a beautifully constructed *Round About Midnight*. There was a trenchant examination of the material, the investigation of the theme's inner recesses, with a proxy control exerted by composer Monk through the unexpected melodic turns of his original tune. Literally on the strength of it, *Life* magazine ran a picture feature on Gillespie and the band in its very next issue, but the emphasis was on their novelty value and not on the musical triumphs.

Such considerations were of little consequence to the trumpeter. It was further publicity and a further aid in his task of selling a music that still found little support outside the specialist jazz followers. He returned to New York in the fall and accepted a residency at the Royal Roost, using much the same line-up as used in California. The band, however, was about to suffer a tragic loss. Chano Pozo had absented himself from a brief Southern stop-over and returned to New York. The circumstances are obscure but it appeared that, following an unresolved altercation at the Rio Bar on 111th Street, Pozo had remained at the bar drinking. The man involved had left the premises only to get a gun and then later returned and wreaked his terrible revenge.

Gillespie was devasted, but life had to go on, and in the next couple of years men such as Sabu Martinez, Bobo Guerra and Carlos Duchesne attempted the impossible task of filling Pozo's shoes. At least, in one sense, it hardly seemed to matter. In an attempt to keep a big band together, Gillespie made more and more compromises. Extensive use was made of the comic value of bop vocals from both himself and Joe Carroll, and the visual aspect of the 'uniform' was done to death.

Ironically, the 1949/50 band itself was very good, and Gillespie has described it as technically the best band he ever had. The reed section with John Coltrane and Jimmy Heath on altos, Paul Gonsalves and Jesse Powell on tenors and Al Gibson on baritone, was especialy strong, and with Willie Cook and Matthew Gee in the brass sections the band could be as good in performance as it was 'on paper'. Unfortunately, material like *You Stole my Wife you Horsethief*, *Carambola* and *Tally Ho* hardly stretched the group's instrumental capabilities, and too often Gillespie was forced to take the easy way out.

For the American nation as a whole it was also a troubled period. On 25 June 1950 North Korean troops launched a full-scale attack on South Korea and within three days had captured the capital at Seoul. President Truman responded immediately and, if only in a numerical sense, American troops fronted the retaliatory action. The story of military miscalculation as the 'United Nations' force pushed past the borders at the 38th Parallel, the Chinese support for the North with 'Mao's volunteers' and the general political backlash ensured that America was involved in the most futile of wars for the best part of three years.

The general involved on the American account was Douglas MacArthur but, as things in Korea went from bad to worse and the accusations and counter-accusations flew between the White House and the battlefield, Truman became more and more disenchanted with his military representative and in March 1951 dismissed MacArthur.

Back home, there was the further complication of McCarthyism. On 9 February Senator Joseph McCarthy alleged that he had the names of more than two hundred 'card-carrying Communists' in the State Deprtment and, in so doing, he disturbed a hornet's nest that disrupted the nation and shattered many people's faith in government. A Subversive Activities Control Board was set up and, despite an attempted block by Truman, it came into existence. The hounding of innocent citizens and the whole 'Reds under the Bed' purge began and it found support in many places. The outcome was that, for some years, Americans suffered a collective uncertainty far worse than that experienced after Pearl Harbor and through World War II.

It was not the climate in which a big band might flourish, and many disbanded at this time. Among the number were Charlie Barnet and Woody Herman, and even the great Count Basie reduced the size of his band to septet proportions in 1950 as the music world reflected the problems in the Senate. Certainly it was neither time nor place for a big band playing music that had still to enjoy national approval.

For Gillespie, however, there were extra-musical problems. He was involved in a road accident in which he had been thrown from his bicycle and slightly injured. A court case followed, in the course of which the trumpeter claimed that his instrumental range had been impaired. Whether the federal court believed it or not, the judges found for Gillespie but awarded what was, in any real terms, a derisory sum. The beneficiary accepted and continued to play with neither visible nor aural difference discernible.

Pressures were nevertheless building up for Gillespie – the band leader. The cost of keeping a seventeen or eighteen piece unit on the road had reached somewhat daunting proportions and the band found itself with fewer bookings to sustain it. Gillespie had begun to resent the concessions he was forced to make and, as further coercion came from home, he reluctantly decided to fold. His final job was in Chicago, and there were scenes of some sadness when the announcement was made.

Gillespie's first record date after the dissolution of the big band was under the Parker banner and with a superb quintet that included Monk, Curley Russell and drummer Buddy Rich. The trumpeter played extremely well and the issue of various takes was of considerable use in weighing the amount of spontaneity involved. The second take of *An Oscar for Treadwell*, for instance, demonstrates just how far he would go to change a solo,. The first take is tidily developed, but the whole thing is refined into a very shapely finished product in the second. That the first attempt begat the second is not in doubt, but the degree of improvement does show that, for all his extempore skills, Gillespie was a thinking musician.

Strangely enough, Gillespie's last recording date in 1950 involved a massive twenty-five piece string supported orchestra. Five times in his career he has fronted 'with strings' sessions, twice with arrangers Joe Boyer and Daniel White in Paris in 1952 and 1953 and three times with Johnny Richards in 1945, 1950 and 1954. The 1950 sessions were, in fact, the most successful in terms of musical cohesion, but it is significant that Gillespie was prepared to make stylistic adjustments to this end.

Richards was a highly experienced musician and a multi-instrumentalist. He had spent much of the thirties writing film music, led his own band for more than five years in the forties and had become associated with 'progressive' jazz when writing arrangements for Stan Kenton. His charts were at times heavily textured and somewhat laboured, but he worked well with both strings and woodwind and, for this exercise, he had eleven strings as well as bassoon, flute, oboe, French horn and harp.

In the event, this army made no attempt to phrase in a jazz manner. The ungainly gait of a 'jazzed' string section was well known to Richards, and he was not about to take his arrangements into that aesthetic cul-de-sac. His approach was predictably about the textures he knew. He provided a cool, swirling backdrop against which Gillespie could act out his own soliloquies and into which he could inject his own dramas.

For Gillespie it was not easy. He could not use his assets to the full, and perhaps his one real frailty was most cruelly exposed. Little demand was put on his amazingly sophisticated harmonic insight and even less on his stunning ability to improvise brilliantly at any tempo. Instead, the limelight was thrown on the one aspect of his playing in which he placed little importance. In his search for creative expansion Gillespie had always regarded 'tone' as a comparatively minor consideration, but there, with the position centre stage, he had no choice but to give priority to the sound he made.

He actually approached the problem in two different ways. The first could be the work of almost any trumpeter, and it occurred at the opening of *Alone Together*. Most of the Gillespie trademarks were missing, the notes were held firmly and the phraseology of bop was tempered to the needs of the background. Above all else, there was a genuine attempt to 'fill out' the tone, show loyalty to the appropriate middle register and ensure that attention was paid to smooth delivery.

In contrast, *What is There to Say* took a second course as it faced the added problem of going into the upper register while still bringing bebop into this musical environment. The different solution took Gillespie's trumpet playing into a musical area that owed much to Harry James in his sentimental *Ciribiribin* guise. There was an attendant paucity of creative ideas, and the piece was concluded with a high-note, spuriously dramatic climax. It was certainly not the setting for Gillespie, but one could not deny that it was the effort made by the trumpeter that gave the music some merit. Without Gillespie, it would have come dangerously near to Palm Court trivia, and it once again posed the question, 'why do jazzmen still experience the old inferiority complex about straight music?' Without them such sessions would be little more than novelty interludes.

CHAPTER 6

COOL BREEZE

To be without a band was hard for Gillespie, but he was not a man afraid of adversity. Not surprisingly, he resented the lay press and its contention that the folding of one orchestra marked the end of bop. That it had become a vital and irrevocable part of the jazz mainstream and that jazz would never again sound the same, had seemed to escape their notice.

In one sense, it was something of a back-handed compliment to the trumpeter, but the scribes concerned were off on their own personal trips to find another musical novelty. As history was to prove, their excursion into the ethereal world of cool jazz gently perverted the course of the music for a couple of years and, in so doing, diverted attention from the major practitioners of the era.

With neither record contract nor place to play on a regular basis, Gillespie went to work as a single. While getting himself together, he fronted various house-rhythm sections and even, for a short period, played at Birdland with Charlie Parker – and another string orchestra. Birdland, in fact, proved something of a place of salvation at the time, and when Gillespie got a group together early in 1951, this is where they mainly played. The group itself, with Coltrane, Jackson, Percy and Jimmy Heath, Blakey and pianist Billy Taylor, was outstanding. Coltrane had switched to tenor and was playing with growing authority and, with the young Blakey beginning to show the fire that was later to ignite the Jazz Messengers, this was a group to hear.

Gillespie was still plotting his career course both in the musial and non-musical sense. Still not satisfied with his treatment in off-stage negotiations, he decided that he would have more control of his own destiny if he had his own record company. In 1951, he went about setting this up and, with the aid of former trucker Dave Usher, Dee Gee records came into being.

The venture endured for less than two years. The first recording

56

session was in March 1951 and the last in July 1952. It was mainly designed to issue records by its owner, but there were other releases by the likes of the Milt Jackson Quartet. Not surprisingly, Gillespie was delighted with his new toy and was quite determined to make it succeed. Therein, however, lay the snare. In an effort to reach as wide an audience as possible, too much emphasis was placed on vocal novelty. The vocals were shared by the leader and Joe Carroll, and disappointingly little was heard of the impressive soloists available.

For his part, Joe 'Bebop' Carroll, a Philadelphian who had taken hipster Leo Watson as his model, was not without talents. Ostensibly a comedy singer, Caroll had a good feeling for jazz in the bop manner, he organised his solos much as might a horn player of the day and, while paying scant attention to the 'significance' of the lyric, built vocal structures full of instrumental logic. With Gillespie, he played his part in the trivial banter and mugging that went on and he added novelties like *Oo-Shoo-Be-Doo-Be* to the group's book.

(l to r) Bill Graham, Joe Carroll, Dizzy Gillespie, Hans Koller and Lou Hackney

Unfortunately, the emerging talent of John Coltrane was soon to be lost to the band. Like his leader, the young saxophonist had always been something of a philosophical thinker and, while in the big band, he had often joined Gillespie in putting the world to rights over a bottle of Johnny Walker Black Label. In the process, they had become good friends, but Coltrane's interest in drugs had developed to the heroin stage by the time the septet had settled in New York, and this circumstance had begun to cause problems for the band. Finally, Gillespie was forced to let him go and, as a replacement, he hired alto and baritone saxophonist Bill Graham.

Despite the worries of his record company and the concessions that were being made on stage and on record, Gillespie was playing well. As a pirate recording of the time shows, he came dangerously near to overpowering the mighty Charlie Parker in the course of a session recorded at Birdland in March 1951, even though his playing was reflecting his need to adjust to the different demands of the small combo.

Despite all of his earlier experience in that field, Gillespie had been fronting a big band non-stop for almost four years. He had become accustomed to using a full ensemble as a backdrop for his forays into the upper register and had become divorced from the very different disciplines of small group playing. His solos had once again to become more than a creative upper stratum; they needed to be organic parts of each performance and much of 1951 was taken in getting this balance right.

The jazz world was introduced to a somewhat changed Gillespie. There was no drastic about-turn in style, but more an adjustment of attitude. Increasingly, he began to 'talk' through his horn, using half-valve notes for emotive effect and using mutes not as an alternative sound to his open horn but as a series of highly varied sounds, each a contrast to the other.

Despite this, Dee Gee releases, in the main, put the emphasis on sales figures, and it was left to reports of live performance to confirm that Gillespie remained a potent musical force. This fact was put into more sharp relief in the spring of 1952 when he again went to Paris and, in the absence of a band of his own, was pleased to become involved in a series of recordings with local American expatriates and the better French players.

Gillespie renewed his musical association with his old Uptown House colleague Don Byas and certainly seemed to relish his work in all of the pick-up combos in which he was involved. Because of the circumstances, he tended to play standards and, with no vocals to worry about, was able to parade talents. The French were still in awe of his astonishing technique, but they were now getting the advantage of his more expansive outlook. Not every tempo was set at breakneck speed and Gillespie was beginning to sound like a more emotionally involved player as he introduced greater tonal variety into every solo.

Obviously, not every club date or record session was a total success and Gillespie could not, once again, resist the temptation to try his hand at a 'with string' venture. This time the exercise was billed as Dizzy Gillespie and His Operatic Strings and the arrangers were Jo Boyer and Daniel White. The Johnny Richards formula was repeated, Gillespie was the featured soloist; three trombones and a jazz rhythm section were used and the orchestra comprised twenty-five pieces, mainly strings. There, all similarity ended, and the aesethic poverty of such fusions was glaringly exposed. The only moments of any artistic validity were those when Gillespie soloed. The backgrounds tended to retard rather than inspire him and, when he sat down, the orchestra offered its effete platitudes as an interlude before his next personal statement. The trumpeter seemed not to notice; he was in his well loved Paris and amongst friends.

Certainly his return to New York was less happy. In his absence, Dee Gee had foundered and, with reluctance, he wound up the company. He had the misfortune to badly injure a jaywalker in a street accident, lost his driving licence and ended up paying a substantial sum in compensation. He was also hit by two spurious paternity suits both of which caused him considerable trouble, to say nothing of the unhappiness at home.

His final disaster came about in the January 1953, although in this case it turned out to be something of a blessing. While playing at a club on New York's 45th Street, he had used his day off to throw a party for Lorraine's birthday celebrations. He had played briefly but, during an intermission, had gone for a breath of fresh air, leaving his trumpet in an upright stand. During his absence, two comedians were pushing each other about as part of their act and, in the course of the horseplay, one fell against Gillespie's horn. Almost as a chance in a million, the bell was bent so that, when the instrument was played in the normal way it pointed toward the ceiling.

Not surprisingly, his friends were almost frightened to tell him, but when he returned to the club he put the horn to his mouth and began to play. In his own words he explained that 'I played it and I liked the sound . . . I remembered the way the sound had come from it, quicker to the ear – to my ear, the player'. He got Lorraine to produce an artist's impression of such a trumpet and instructed his horn manufacturers to produce one like it.

They did, and within months he had changed to the then unique design permanently. He further explained that 'One of the things a horn like mine remedies is the problem of holding your instrument too far down when you're reading music. You can never hold this

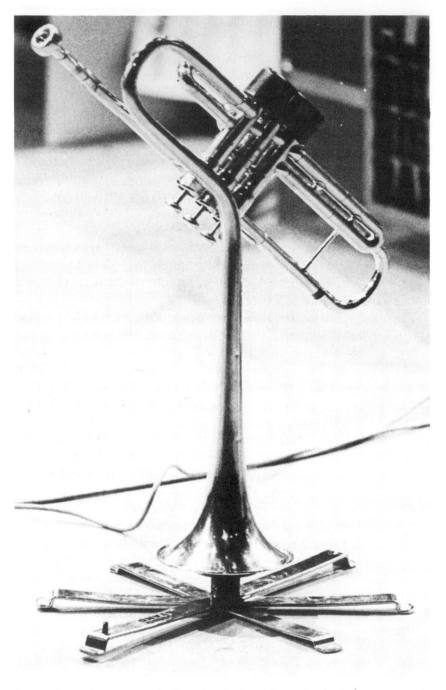

The bent horn

horn down low enough for the bell of it to be below the music stand.'

From the audience standpoint, there was no complaint, there was certainly a greater dissemination of sound and, if anything, an increased sense of clarity. Initially, it was also a visual novelty, and it was destined to become a Gillespie trade-mark long after the berets and bop glasses were forgotten.

60

In fact his last tour using the old horn came immediately after this incident and was to Europe. On the trip, he gave the operatic strings idea a further try, with results no less dire than in the previous year but in the main he was working with a group that he had brought from America.

The tour began successfully in Scandinavia, but a band with Wade Legge on piano, Lou Hackney on bass, Al Jones on drums and only saxophonist Bill Graham to share the solo duties was hardly an all-star band. Furthermore, it included vocalist Joe Carroll and this ensured a surfeit of novelty vocals and comedy routines.

Fortunately, the French Vogue company were keen to record them and, by the time they reached Paris, they had the backing of audiences for whom Gillespie could do no wrong. This was borne out in no uncertain terms whne the Vogue company so graphically captured the atmosphere of a concert in front of a capacity crowd at the Salle Pleyel.

Gillespie walked out to a rapturous ovation, wearing a light suit and with a corned-beef tartan beret that made him look like a twenty-four handicap golfer on his first trip to St Andrews. Carroll's reception was somewhat less ecstatic, and this was certainly not the best band that the trumpeter had ever led. Nevertheless, the audience papered over the cracks for themselves, laughed in most of the right places and seemed determined to clap good and poor solos alike. Most of the more pedestrian moments came from Graham, and it is perhaps significant that early record issues of the concert were drastically butchered to hide the less palatable musical truths.

The concert also seemed to highlight another important department of Gillespie's musical arsenal. In such an all action sextet, there was no longer room for the luxury of a specialist conga drummer and, in the circumstances, the leader became a very willing stand-in. He had absorbed the lessons of Chano Pozo well and, on a title like *Swing Low, Sweet Cadillac*, he showed how subtle, swinging and rhythmically unpredictable he could be. In many ways, this is an underplayed aspect of Gillespie's amazing all round skills and it was to be one that he was to develop in later years, perhaps as a welcome rest for his 'chops' but none the less as a major part of his musical armament.

Being in Europe was certainly no hardship for Gillespie, but there were other reasons why he should wish to be away from the American scene. Late in 1952, baritone saxophonist Gerry Mulligan began a series of recordings featuring a quartet that included trumpeter Chet Baker, either Bob Whitlock or Carson Smith on bass and Chico Hamilton on drums. While they were hardly inspired, they did have a certain clean cut style, the solos were simplistic and the rhythm had an almost Dixieland-like bounce.

Amazingly, the records they made attracted a cult following; scribes linked them stylistically to the Miles Davis Capitol sessions of 1949/50 and the word Cool was coined to cover their unpretentious but undoubtedly coy demeanour. It was no conspiracy on the part of Mulligan or Baker, but it presaged a move toward the discreet rather than the verbose, the over polite rather than the natural and the genteel rather than the powerful.

For some time, the recording world was centred in California and certain subversive critics began to suggest that Cool jazz had replaced bop and that its carefully studied manner was in some way superior. History was repeating itself, and here was another homogenized version of black jazz, touted as better and available to middle brow, middle class America.

In various interviews, Gillespie was not as outspoken as he might have been. He tended to concentrate his comments on the virility of black music and to draw attention to its more swinging identity. In fact, he answered the challenge in the best way possible. Almost immediately on his return across the Atlantic, he took part in a concert that was to be hailed as the high spot of his career to that date.

A Canadian Jazz Society had booked both Parker and himself for a concert at Toronto's Massey Hall, but someone within their ranks came up with the idea of hiring pianist Bud Powell, bassist Charles Mingus and drummer Max Roach and of billing the group as *The Quintet Of The Year*. Few could have argued with such a title but, bearing in mind the number of such all-star groups that have failed to live up to expectations, the five men must have experienced some concern as they took to the stage.

These feelings were not entirely misplaced; the outcome fell somewhere between the career highspot suggested by some observers and the slightly disorganised jam session implied by others. Such arguments were possible only because a recording was made of the proceedings. Unknown to his colleagues, Mingus had secreted his tape recorder into the hall. This was not done out of personal interest in the music but as a conscious plan to get a recording that could be issued later on his own Debut record label.

In the event, a great deal of outstanding jazz was played, the audience identified with it, and their enthusiasm flooded across the footlights. At times their fervent support had a disruptive effect, directing Gillespie, in particular, into more excitable areas. On balance, however, it added to the atmosphere and was more of a help than a hindrance.

The real chicanery began only when the concert was over and well before the original record was issued. Tape splices were evident in *Salt Peanuts* and it was claimed that Mingus had deliberately throttled back on his contribution throughout, in order that he might superimpose some of the bass lines in the studio afterwards. Finally, a title not recorded at Massey Hall and featuring Gillespie, Parker and Mingus, but with Billy Taylor and Art Taylor in place of Powell and Roach, was added to the roster of titles issued!

In the circumstances, a detailed examination of this recording is more than justified. The praise that had been heaped on the date and the questions posed by the mysteries surrounding the subsequent adjustments, demand some explanations. In terms of jazz and pop recordings made in the sixties and beyond, the later modifications would have been acceptable. In 1953, they were not, and the performance must finally be judged by what happened on the night.

Parker was certainly not pleased when the circumstances of the recording became known and he later expressed reservations about the issue of such a warts-and-all performance. One cannot help but feel that such caution was misplaced. By almost any other standards, the jazz produced was of the highest quality. Powell was at his most lucid, what was heard of Mingus was authoritative and the immaculate Roach was going through the full drum spectrum. More significantly, Gillespie and Parker had played with a passion that made their position as the leaders of the 1953 avant-garde unassailable.

Certainly such performances made nonsense of any self doubt but, for the players involved, 'Cool Jazz', as sold by the media, posed a threat. Perhaps it was symptomatic of an American nation washing its dirty linen in public by trying to 'clean up' its arts. A society terrified of Reds-under-the-Bed wanting to revert to the Hollywood High School undershirt image. The virility of the ghetto arts, albeit played in Carnegie Hall, was at odds with that ideal in 1953.

In retrospect, Gillespie's next career move can be seen as a result of that situation. He signed for Jazz at the Philharmonic boss Norman Granz, became part of the impressario's touring JATP circus and thereby found himself in a totally different, musical environment.

Granz, born in Los Angeles, California, had attended UCLA and, after working as a clerk on the Los Angeles Stock Exchange, did war-time army service. He worked briefly in the film industry but his enthusiasm for jazz led him to try his hand at concert promotion. By the time that Gillespie signed, JATP had become a universally famous organisation and its creator had very strong feelings about how it should be run.

Seen from the point of view of the artists who worked for him in

1953, Granz represented genuine security. He treated musicians with respect and was totally without racial prejudice. He was, moreover, determined that there were no unsurmountable stylistic barriers in jazz and that players of all musical persuasions could work together if given time to adjust.

Norman Granz

The amazing thing was that total disasters were very rare and, at the time, most musicians were prepared to accept such challenges in return for a regular pay cheque and a socially congenial working atmosphere. The touring was arduous but they did travel in style and for the extrovert players the rivalry was a stimulation to be enjoyed. Granz traded in excitement, he recreated the jazz sessions of the forties and he expected his musicians to respond. In Dizzy Gillespie he had one perfectly equipped so to do.

Granz also believed in getting the most from the available talent and, because of this, his most favoured piano solost of the period, Oscar Peterson, also became the central figure in his house rhythm section. The choice proved to be perfect. JATP had soloists from many stylistic backgrounds, swing era giants weaned on the four even beats of a Count Basie-type rhythm section, cool school saxophonists at home with brush dominated unobstrusiveness, and

Oscar Peterson with Norman Granz (seated)

moderns, like Gillespie, who would have thrived on the angularity of a stabbing, bop piano and bomb-dropping drummer.

It implies no criticism of Peterson to say that he rapidly became all things to all men. His own solo technique, inspired by the flowing rhetoric of Art Tatum, had had the corners sharpened by his contact with the boppers. He could play a rolling blues but his playing could also adopt a hard edge if need arose. In fact, his musical relationship with Gillespie proved to be highly productive.

Ben Webster told Steve Voce (*Jazz Journal International*, 1967) that 'The best accompanying pianist I ever had was Oscar Peterson. He listens to the horn men and seems to know exactly what they're going to play, and sets it up for them instinctively.' That situation was no less true for Gillespie and, although the trumpeter's demands would have been as far from Webster's as it is possible to imagine, Peterson wrought a different kind of magic. The pianist laid foundations that were at times as decorative as the musical structures they supported but then only as obtrusive as seemed decent.

The presence of Peterson ensured that Granz's musicians could almost forget the backgrounds and could concentrate on their

65

Dizzy Gillespie with Oscar Peterson, Tiffany Club, Los Angeles, 1950s

more specialized duels. In this area, things were not always as well balanced, but it was Gillespie's battle with his peers that concern us here. The best was undoubtedly with his mentor Roy Eldridge. Gillespie has said that he was *shaped* by the Pittsburgh firebrand's horn, but this did not stop them from engaging in near mortal combat.

What surprises newcomers is that only six years separates them in age but it was just enough to give an 'old man – new boy' angle to the musical argument. In reality, they were very good friends and their musical meetings only rarely became 'carving contests'. It is just something in the soul of all trumpeters that seems to drive them to be top men. For two such giants to be locked in battle usually meant that Granz and the audiences got what they wanted.

It could take the form of a Gillespie riff backing for a powerful Eldridge statement, a simple background figure from Eldridge to stir a Gillespie flight or just a straight four bar chase passage. A trivial tune like *Pretty Eyed Baby* could feature their idiosyncratic scat singing, each providing an obbligato more interesting than the vocal line.

Not all of the musical challenges were as productive, and some failed when success seemed the most likely outcome. Despite the fact that tenor saxophonist Stan Getz used what was ostensibly the same jazz vernacular, his style set up totally different and less easily resolved problems. When Gillespie had enjoyed a brief spell with JATP in 1946, he had worked amicably with Charlie Parker, Willie Smith and Lester Young, three very contrasting players.

With Getz, however, there seemed to be an edge, a rivalry that transcended normal competition.

On sessions that involved only those two players or perhaps one other horn, tempos seemed to be uniformly inappropriate for Getz. For Gillespie, a fast treatment was ideal for his densely arpeggiated line, but on titles like *It Don't Mean a Thing* from (1953) or *Be-bop* or *Wee* (from 1956), Getz sounded leaden footed after Gillespie's high-stepping commentary. For a brief time in this part of his career, Getz was beginning to believe the critics. He was 'roughing up' his act, but the musical stance he took did not suit him and a Crow/Jim attitude pleased Gillespie no more than would have the alternative.

Tenors, however, were good companions for fifties Gillespie.

Dizzy with Shorty Rogers and Stan Getz

The Sonny Rollins partnership was particularly productive. The young Rollins was just emerging, and the opportunity of working with the all confident trumpeter seemed to act as a spur. Instead of trying to match Gillespie in detail, Rollins used the more demanding tempos as a springboard for his most daring and wayward excursions.

If only because of his allegiance to Parker, Sonny Stitt was another who fitted the Gillespie mould as easily as might have been expected. In contrast, Paul Gonsalves did so while remaining staunchly true to his own style, and the same was largely true of Coleman Hawkins. His case, however, was somewhat unique and it was conditioned by the fact that, in the middle fifties, he was playing with a new expansiveness. This meant that he was never completely prepared to surrender centre stage to anybody, although with Gillespie, he usually seemed willing to share it.

Unfortunately, JATP concerts of the period could become rather predictable as Granz, formally the champion of the jam sessions, began encouraging his players to produce individual horn solos built into a medley. It was a policy that underemployed his superb roster of soloists and tended to force even the most creative players into producing note for note reproductions of well loved improvisational lines.

Gillespie was not tied religiously to JATP, however, and the fifties saw him involved in various international projects as well as still being a willing night-club performer. Perhaps the most singularly important event was his 1956 State Department tour. Black politician Adam Clayton Powell Jr. had recommended Gillespie to President Dwight D. Eisenhower and had persuaded him on the wisdom of a flag waving tour of Africa, the Near East and Asia.

The reason for the tour was never really disguised. Eisenhower, who came to power in January 1953, was the ultimate rags-to-riches president. His politics took very much the middle line, and although this was not always his own choice, he responded to the situation. The Democrats removed the slim Republican margin in Congress by 1954 and, for six of his eight years in office, Eisenhower had to function with a Congress controlled by the opposing party.

The civil rights issue had become very important. The Supreme Court had left no doubt about the country's stance on inequality with its unanimous 1954 *Brown* v *Board of Education of Topeka* ruling. This was given further endorsement in 1955 when it was decreed that immediate implementation was required. The time was obviously right for the president to give his nod of approval and to show to the world that America's racial problems were over.

In choosing Gillespie as his ambassador, however, he had not   *Dizzy Gillespie*

made the most perfect choice. The trumpeter deliberately ducked his pre-tour briefing and made clear to his intimates that he was not about to go to the old world and lie about his blissful circumstances at home. What he was prepared to do was to spread a little happiness in the company of a big band financed by somebody else and taking no racial, religious or sexual stance.

Gillespie missed more than the briefing and was not on hand to rehearse the band. While he was touring Europe, that chore fell to band members Quincy Jones, Melba Liston and Ernie Wilkins, but in a very short time they had a well-organised, fifteen-piece unit on their hands. Singers Herb Lance and Dottie Salters made up the full complement, and the leader further swelled their number when he joined the party in Rome.

Right from the start, the tour was affected by political issues. The opening in Bombay was cancelled and instead the band opened in Iran (then Persia). From then on, the tour stayed in countries that had U.S. military bases or an extremely friendly relationship with the United States.

For Gillespie, it was a social honeymoon. While he was not prepared to be a propagandist, he was more than willing to integrate with the local communities. At many venues he gave away concert tickets; in Karachi he sat alongside a snake charmer and did his own reptile beguiling act with his muted and up-turned trumpet. He listened to a considerable amount of ethnic music and sat in with the local musicians. He continually cocked a snoot at authority and showed an endless determination to play for the man-in-the-street and not for the privileged minorities.

Inevitably, the music was not always understood, but Gillespie did not insult the audiences by compromise. In the end, it was his friendly demeanour, obvious enthusiasm and willingness to include his audiences in the atmosphere of the concert that won the day. In Yugoslavia one crowd even tried to join the band on stage. Ultimately, one must acknowledge that more real good had been done for international harmony than would ever have been achieved by a pompous man of letters.

Nevertheless Gillespie, ever the opportunist, did not hesitate to send Eisenhower a wire on his return, part of which read, 'Jazz is our own American folk music that communicates with all peoples regardless of language or social barriers. I urge you to do all in your power to continue exploiting this valuable form of American expression of which we are so proud' (reported by Stanley Dance in *Jazz Journal*, October 1956).

The President certainly took notice. When Gillespie returned, Eisenhower invited him to the White House Correspondents' Dinner in what proved to be a name-dropper's delight. More significantly, he sanctioned another tour, this time to South

Dizzy with Vic Ash and
Buck Clayton

America. Before going, however, Gillespie provided documented evidence of the tour by recording with the full linc-up for Granz. The results were good, and Quincy Jones's superb arrangement of *Yesterdays*, in particular, showed how much attention was paid to fine detail.

The record was made in New York, but despite its undoubted quality, it suffered a rather mixed reception in the media. Yet another return to the past was under way in America, as a jazz world, still suspicious of bop and more than a little sated by the New Orleans revival, looked back to the swing era giants. Many of these players had been caught up in the cross fire of the extremists. They had been unjustifiably ignored and had in many cases been forced to compromise just to earn a living.

Their return to the centre stage was especially welcome, and men like Buck Clayton, Vic Dickenson, Buddy Tate and Ed Hall began to get recording opportunities commensurate with their considerable abilities. Unfortunately, this return to thirties style 'mainstream' did not promote only good. The movement lent

71

power to the anti-bop lobby and some of the musicians involved took time out to snipe at other styles. There were still many musicians who failed to grasp the fact that bop was a vital part of the jazz mainstream. They did not see that it had entered the very fabric of the music's evolutionary progress and missed no chance to critizise its leading practitioners. Cornettist Ruby Braff, a gifted young newcomer to the mainstream scene, showed exceptional skills with his horn but reactionary attitudes with the pen. Reviewing the State Department band he said, 'I cannot take seriously a solo that doesn't in some way utilize the wisdom of Armstrong. Such work, in my estimation, will always show a lack of culture' (*Saturday Review*).

While ignoring the fact that anyone who chooses to use the word 'utilize' when he means 'use' must himself be culturally suspect, Braff is also guilty of the most blinkered line of thinking. Certainly Gillespie was no Armstrong copyist, but to 'use the wisdom of Armstrong' was just what he did, albeit in a style that was two generations from its source. The influence's most direct route may have come from the Armstrong style, most evident when he was fronting a big band, but there can be no doubting the origins of the early Gillespie style. Had Braff listened more constructively to the *Groovin'* track on the album in question, he would have appreciated the strong, umbilical link with Armstrong's 1931 *Shine*, 1936 *Swing that Music or* 1983 *Jubilee*.

Not surprisingly, Braff's opinions were of little consequence to Gillespie, and with the very welcome Presidential nod, the trumpeter set out for his second important tour. In terms of his own edification, it was even more satisfying than the first. His affinity with Latin rhythms made the prospect especially inviting, and it was hardly surprising that he found Brazil particularly exciting.

He visited various samba schools, a mini-carnival was put on in his honour, and he danced and played with the locals whenever he could. In Argentina, he donned a gaucho costume and rode on horseback through the streets, and he met pianist composer-arranger Lalo Schifrin. Musically the tour was a success, and it was inevitable that titles such as *Manteca* and *Cubana Be* were popular with the locals. Gillespie's amazingly approachable manner made him welcome wherever the band played, but it was a two way thing, and he returned to New York with his love of South America permanently cemented.

CHAPTER 7

SCHOOL DAYS

Shortly after his return Gillespie played before twenty thousand at the first New York Jazz Festival at Randall's Island. He had been able to keep the State Department big band together, at least for that event, and he received a tumultuous reception.

Ironically, it was before a very much smaller audience that the next part of the Gillespie story unfolded. For three weeks in August 1957 he joined the faculty of the School of Jazz at Lenox, Massachusetts. The idea had begun at the Music Inn, a commuter's retreat in the pleasant Berkshire district of Lenox, that had become something akin to the old-style European rhythm club. For some time lectures had been given and discussion groups interested in jazz had been encouraged to meet in the relaxed atmosphere.

Pianist John Lewis was the brains behind the idea. In the previous year he had held a seminar with guests including Sonny Rollins and veteran trombonist Wilbur De Paris. Such was the success that Lewis decided to set up the school, and in 1957 he recruited, amongst others, Gillespie, Milt Jackson, Oscar Peterson, Max Roach, Jimmy Giuffre and Jim Hall. Critic Marshall Stearns and folklorist Willis James from Spellman College in Georgia were added, and the curriculum embraced group playing, composition and arranging, as well as lectures on jazz history.

Students and faculty alike stayed in Wheatleigh Hall, the home of the Boston Symphony Orchestra's summer school and the inspiration for Gillespie's later composition *Wheatleigh Hall*. The classes included instruction in ensemble playing, in which students were given the chance to play with their own particular idol. The arranging side of the operation was conducted by Bill Russo and made considerable demands on the aspiring young musician, but what surprised many students was the scope and detail of the historical lectures.

For faculty members their participation at the school represented a rest from one night whistle stops and the hassle of night club playing, but its timetable came as something of a culture shock. Gillespie was reported in *Harper's Magazine* as saying 'Eight in the morning, I can't lift an alarm clock and my chops, man, I can't even find 'em.' The truth was, however, that the trumpeter enjoyed his stay there. His opening instruction, 'In jazz, if you can't sing it, you can't play it' became something of a rallying cry of the whole course, and Gillspie did his own share of adapting. Nat Hentoff (*Jazz Monthly*, April 1958) told of a situation in which trumpet coach Gillespie was faced with a student whose tone he actively disliked. The young aspirant liked the particular sound, however, and as a result Gillespie set about helping him to perfect it. The course was not intended to produce clones but it was rather regarded as an open door to self expression.

Back to the reality of being a practising jazz musician, Gillespie still had the backing of Granz and his record company. This meant that, although he still had contact with the State Department band, he could accept concert dates or record for Verve. He was also free to play on any speciality recording date that might appeal to either himself or Granz. One such session teamed him with the unlikely Stuff Smith, the violinist once dubbed by critic Timmie Rosenkrantz as the 'palpitating Paganini'. The outcome was surprisingly good. Coming from diametrically opposed, musical directions and prompted by totally different rhythmic needs, Gillespie and Smith somehow managed to strike just the right sparks from each other. The tandem journey was not entirely untroubled but, like his work with Eldridge, Hawkins and Gonsalves, it showed that Gillespie's roots ran deeper than his opponents contended. There were still perceptive observers, in sympathy with Gillespie's style, who retained nagging reservations about the content of his solos. They were worried that instrumental pyrotechnics were a drug to which he was irrevocably hooked and, without realising it, were endorsing the view held by the establishment opposition.

Very often the observations of a critic, antagonistic toward a musician, can throw important light on the man concerned. The occasionally annoying, but often dangerously perceptive, Stanley Dance wrote of a performance in the hit-or-miss atmosphere of a 1957 JATP concert (*Jazz Journal*, July 1957) that 'Dizzy has little follow through, little continuity and when he bothers to finish his sentences, he seems to have said *something of no importance in the most complicated fashion*.

On the face of it, this is an outrageous statement but it was made in the reaction to the record label hyperbole that christened one of Gillespie's 1957 records as *The Greatest Trumpet Of Them All*. The

Dizzy Gillespie in London with Lord Montague and various musicians, including Ken Colyer (left), Bud Freeman, Buck Clayton and Humphrey Lyttelton

74

Dizzy with Shorty Rogers, Stan Getz and Jimmy Giuffre

truth, as is always the case, lay somewhere between the two extreme points of view. Certainly in the past Gillespie had given Dance cause to accuse him of verbosity, but the trumpeter was never as devoid of improvisational inspiration as the Englishman suggested. It would have been more constructive to have recognised that certain solos were indigestibly rich in multi-vitamin ideas.

Strangely enough, *The Greatest Trumpet* album went some way toward presenting the opposite view. As the fifties had progressed, Gillespie, finding himself increasingly in small JATP jam session situations or leading his own small combos, had adapted himself to the needs of the new surroundings. The ability to accommodate an erring colleague or to cover for his own temporary loss of direction became second nature to him. The listener became increasingly aware of his greater sense of relaxation of what he might himself describe as *cool*.

Solos on titles like *Reminiscing* and *Just By Myself* told of his continued instrumental mastery but there was a more highly developed, emotional input. The rhythmically adventurous stance and the unpredictable creative process remained a constant, but these elements were tempered with a sense of complete involvement. There was also a twelve bar blues to show his natural response to the deceptive simplicity of the genre and to the riff based implications of its formula. Gillespie had long since acquired the technical mastery of his horn: the late fifties saw him adding a degree of restraint.

This writer heard Gillespie in live performance for the first time on the 1958 JATP tour of Britain. The Gaumont State Cinema in London's Kilburn was not the ideal concert hall, but the line-up was suitably impressive. In the event, one was prepared to be uncritical, but it was unnecessary. Few of the giants had feet of clay, and Sonny Stitt and Coleman Hawkins played quite superbly.

Stan Getz was something of a disappointment, and in retrospect, it must be said that Gillespie produced a set that did little to tax the musical imagination of the audience. He played with his customary skill but, unlike *The Greatest Trumpet* recording, failed to get fully under the music's skin despite showing himself as a true stylist.

This was also true of his social demeanour. Nevil Skrimshire (*Jazz Journal*, July 1958) toured with the band on behalf of his employers, E.M.I. Records, and he reported that, throughout the tour, Gillespie dressed in a completely brown outfit, even down to the boots. He added that this attire was always crowned by the wearing of a black bowler hat.

Gillespie's more dizzy side was seen when, during one of the interminable coach journeys, he challenged Norman Granz to a running race. His 'guvner' accepted, the wager was set at £5 and a suitable street 'course' was found. The entire JATP entourage was the audience. Granz came second, Gillespie third and Sonny Stitt, the pace maker and medical adviser, a comfortable first.

Gillespie had become something of a chess buff. He carried around a portable set and thought nothing of challenging complete strangers to a game. Skrimshire reported that he experienced mixed fortunes but pointed out, to put the matter in proper perspective, that English band leader Laurie Gold's twelve-year-old son Michael beat Dizzy at the first attempt.

After his return to America Gillespie's earliest experience as a master-of-ceremonies was similarly mixed. The 1958 Monterey Festival took place in October, and the brilliant trumpeter did a pretty appalling job. He became confused with musicians' names and was occasionally absent when announcements were required. Fortunately, he was on hand to introduce Louis Armstrong, whom

he generously described as 'The King'. In view of their past differences, this was something of a welcome olive branch, but there remained the feeling that Gillespie was less than dedicated to the job in hand. He even sported an Oriental skull cap when taking part in a jazz forum with Armstrong, Ralph Gleason and Albert McCarthy, and throughout the three days event his behaviour was essentially dizzy.

Gillespie's differences with Armstrong dated from earlier days and were greatly exaggerated by the media. In fact, the two became increasingly friendly, and in 1959 they were more than happy to share a Timex Jazz TV Show. In it they did their *Umbrella Man* comedy routine, but the amazing thing was that they jelled musically, producing some extremely successful counterpoint for two trumpets. This would certainly not have been a surprise to critic Dan Morganstern who had reported (*Jazz Journal* May 1958) that, in the previous year, he had seen Gillespie dep for Charlie Shavers in a front line that had included Coleman Hawkins and Tony Parenti. The style required had been very much nearer to the Satchmo image, but Gillespie had played a twenty-minute *Royal*

Dizzy Gillespie's quintet at Streatham Astoria, 1969: Leo Wright (alto saxophone), Dizzy (trumpet), Art Davis (double bass) and Teddy Stewart (drums)

Garden Blues 'that would have ranked with his greatest performances'.

Such serious musical exploits were not always fully appreciated, and Gillespie still found himself the victim of marketing men. A 1959 album was released under the title *Have Trumpet, Will Excite*, a play on the then-popular TV Western *Have Gun, Will Travel*. The record was made for Verve so one must suspect the Granz hand in the selecton of the name but as is so often the case with his involvement, the music was far better than the inane title might suggest.

Made by Gillespie's working group at the time the record included Chicago pianist Junior Mance and Les Spann who doubled on guitar and flute. The relationship between the more 'contained' Gillespie and superbly relaxed and blues based Mance flourished, and British audiences had a chance to examine it at first hand when the group that starred in the Newport Jazz Festival package visited Europe in the fall.

Mance's playing was a far cry from the crisp, right-handed bop style of the forties. He belonged to the rolling-blues-based Chicago school that sired Richard Abrahams (later Muhal Richard Abrams) and Jodie Christian. It had a more legato emphasis and it seemed to fit Gillespie's thinking at the time. Lorraine Gillespie had suggested the inclusion of *Moonglow* in a programme of head arrangements, and, perhaps in deference to her, Dizzy played with a rare lyricism. The whole record had a casual air, but the quality of the collective playing confirmed the musicians' familiarity with one another.

CHAPTER 8

THE CHAMP

Gillespie's mother died in 1959 at the age of seventy-four. This had a great effect on him and caused him to re-examine, not only his music, but also his politics and his stance on racism. Musically, he was happy with his combo. Altoist and flautist Leo Wright replaced Spann early in 1960 and, in time for his summer tour of Europe, Lalo Schifrin, the man he had met in Argentina, took over the piano chair. Gillespie, however, was not entirely satisfied and, as part of his self re-evaluation, was trying to move his own jazz beyond the club and festival merry-go-round. He had presented a programme of his compositions at New York's Circle in the Square and a series of Jazz Profiles at The Museum of Modern Art.

He also got together with arranger Clare Fischer to present an entire album dedicated to the music of Duke Ellington. He accepted the fact that this would mean that one of jazz's most extrovert, heart-on-sleeve soloists would be playing the music of the ultimate impressionist, but his instinct was correct. There was no clown's nose behind the veil. The band, including five woodwind, three French horns and a tuba, was chosen with care and the outcome was impressive. There was little doubt that Fischer aspired to the kind of textural densities produced by Gil Evans on albums like the 1957 *Miles Ahead* with Miles Davis. The reason that he never fully achieved this end was that, unlike Davis, Gillespie was not prepared to subjugate his role to that of an ensemble voice, even for a moment. On Billy Strayhorn's lovely *Chelsea Bridge* and Ellington's *Come Sunday* he came near, but Fischer finally had to settle for backgrounds that were complimentary to the material and capable of providing a cushion for the declamatory Gillespie.

This had always been the trumpeter's strength and, whether worrying a blues like *Things Ain't What They Used To Be*, proudly strutting along on *Caravan* or coercing the *Sophisticated Lady* to misbehave he was, however slightly, a man apart from the collective sound. This was never more true than on *Concerto for Cootie*. Like the 1940 original with Cootie Williams, the Fischer/Gillespie version was a total trumpet showcase and use was made of Dizzy's open and muted horn. There the similarity ended, as Gillespie, almost self consciously restrained, presented a completely different improvisational method and escorted the theme down vastly different routes.

If anything, his next project was even more amibitious. Schifrin composed a suit called *Gillespiana* and scored it for a twenty-one-piece orchestra. It represented a complete contrast to the Ellington exercise and, although a highly effective piece, it was damned by faint praise at the time. Verve recorded it over three days in November 1960 and employed quality brass men like Clark Terry, Ernie Royal, Joe Wilder, Urbie Green and Britt Woodman. Schifrin's score astutely pandered to the soloists, but most especially, provided a challenge to the principal. Its *Prelude* offered him a chance to spit fire and a blues section encouraged him to extend himself, while *Pan American* gave his mighty rhythm section licence to cut loose. *Africana* had Gillespie's warmest solo, but Schifrin's arrangements seemed to capture the appropriate mood for each section.

Unfortunately, his piano playing in the working quintet was less appropriate. Its studied air suggested a book-taught jazzman, and although the themes from *Gillespiana* enriched the group's book, Schifrin's readings of them were over formal. In contrast, altoist Wright fitted perfectly. His style, somewhat between Parker's effortless bop and Louis Jordan's fiercely agitated blues, was ideal for the 1961 Gillespie unit and, with Bob Cunningham on bass and Chuck Lampkin on drums, they put considerable collective emphasis on their rhythmic propulsion.

In addition to places like the Museum of Modern Art, the quintet also played the clubs. At San Francisco's Jazz Workshop Gillespie broke house records and while there he showed that his reputation as dizzy was not to be surrendered because of his growing social conscience. Ralph J. Gleason told (sleeve of *An Electrifying Evening*, Verne (J) MV 2605) how 'he reigned nightly in his Nigerian tribal robes and beaded cap' and of how 'he walked the guests to the door and got out on the sidewalk and brought new ones in.'

The quintet, briefly augmented by Joe Carroll, was a great success at the 1961 Monterey Festival where it appeared on the same programme with the new John Coltrane group including Eric Dolphy. Writing in *Down Beat*, Don De Michael described Gillespie's set as the highlight of the festival, and the trumpeter included a performance of Antonio Carlos Jobin's *Desafinado*

*Dizzy Gillespie with
Leonard Feather, Monterey
1961*

which, in Portuguese, means 'sightly out of tune'. The treatment it
received was certainly free of any such fault, but it did draw
attention to the considerable influence that Gillespie had had on
the popularisation of the bossa nova movement. The Monterey
Festival took place five months before this tune was recorded by
Stan Getz.

Immediately after the Monterey events, the quintet travelled,
with the Coltrane unit, to Europe. This writer caught the package

at the Walthamstow Odeon, an art deco cinema in London's suburbia. The thirty minute Coltrane version of *Favourite Things* had left me drained and on this occasion perhaps, deflected me from a true evaluation of the other act. For his part, Gillespie was certainly disadvantaged by a recent change of drummer. Lampkin had been replaced for the tour by Mel Lewis, and his undoubted big band skills were not ideally placed in a quintet committed to rhythms from mixed ethnic sources. Nevertheless, both Gillespie and Wright played beautifully. They included parts of *Gillespiana* in their section of the concert but found that coming on after a nerve-tearing set by Coltrane at his most intense was hardly the perfect arrangement.

On his return to America Gillespie learned that his friend, counsellor and record producer Norman Granz had sold his Verve company to MGM for a considerable sum of money. Dizzy's response was merely to move over to the Philips label.

With more serious matters on his mind in the past, however, he had tended to make light of provocations that he had experienced while working in overtly racist areas. He had done so in part because, for a working musician, retaliation could have been counter-productive, as well as being a serious distraction from the job in hand. There were limits, however, and a brief chain of events had set him on a course of 'stand up and be counted' action.

Tulane University of New Orleans had earlier cancelled one of his concerts, claiming that a local ordinance forbade mixed-race groups. Granz had backed Gillespie to the hilt, against such stupidity, but it was one incident in a stream of events that strengthened Dizzy's resolve to fight all forms of racial bigotry.

Granz further assisted the cause by ensuring that all performance contracts contained non-segregation clauses, and he also helped Gillespie to expose the fact that, even in 1961, there were still segregated musician's union branches. Five years had elapsed since Autherine Lucy had become the first black person to register at the University of Alabama. It had been four years since Orval Faubus had called out the national guard, not to escort black students into the schools of Little Rock, Arkansas, but to enforce their absence. Much had still to be done.

John F. Kennedy had become president elect in 1960 and had done so by the smallest margin in the twentieth century. Many thought that a slight shift in the black vote had been crucial and that this had been brought about by Kennedy's prompt and sympathetic treatment of Dr. Martin Luther King Jr., who had been sentenced on a technicality to four months of hard labour. With the help of his brother Robert F. Kennedy, John Kennedy had secured his release and, in the process, made many new black friends.

Despite this, many thought that the new president's reactions to the ongoing civil-rights programme were somewhat tardy. He tried not to alienate Southern Democrats but he did make some important black appointments. Thurgood Marshall of the NAACP entered the U.S. Circuit Court, Robert Weaver headed the Housing and Home Finance Agency, and Carl Rowan became the Ambassador to Finland.

Gillespie's own racial stance had always been mature. His stand on equality was rightly inflexible but it did not translate to self destructive race hatred. He had many respected white friends and had always acknowledged the importance of his white dominated audiences. He had never hesitated in employing white sidemen and, as an internationalist, was delighted to have a man like Schifrin writing for him in a style that transcended the American jazz ethic.

Schifrin had been particulary active on Gillespie's behalf, and 1962 saw the completion of *The New Continent*. Hollywood was chosen as the venue for a recording of the new work, and mainly West Coast musicians were used. The outcome provided a permanent record of a melodically strong and well-integrated work. The composer had given it unity by the strategic use of melodic extensions and thematic recapitulations. Inevitably the immaculate collective skills of the Californian players were well demonstrated but there were ponderous moments, and these tended to force the trumpeter into the role of virtuoso rather than thoughtfully creative soloist.

Unfortunately, the session marked something of a turning point for Schifrin who, attracted by the compositional possibilities outside jazz, left Gillespie to take on film and TV studio work. His replacement was Kenny Barron. Even more significantly, James Moody, a Gillespie sideman as early as 1946, rejoined the group on what turned out to be a permanent basis. All of these events took place in 1962.

Some time earlier, his booking agents had printed 'Dizzy Gillespie for President' pins. They had done so with humorous intent and purely for publicity. The idea had amused Gillespie and at the time, of course, he had regarded the whole exercise as a joke.

Nevertheless, 1963 saw him becoming increasingly involved in politics and, together with impresario George Wein, he took part in a TV progamme in which youngsters could question their elders. Many of their queries examined the lack of opportunities available to Negroes and they were pleased that Gillespie had spoken of action.

With the 1964 national election campaign looming, it was time to look at the candidates. John F. Kennedy was assassinated on 22

November 1962 and Lyndon Baines Johnson, the vice-president, was sworn in immediately. He was soon faced with the defence of his post and his Republican opponent was Senator Barry Goldwater of Arizona. Goldwater was a conservative who had voted against the civil-rights bill and exploited the 'redneck' backlash of favouring the 'freedom not to associate'. At a Republican meeting he declared that 'Extremism in the defence of liberty is no vice'.

That such a man could be considered for the presidency worried Gillespie enormously, and when jazz writer Ralph Gleason suggested that Dizzy himself had better credentials for the job, he began to take the idea seriously. Gleason began to use his jazz column to promote his possible candidate. He pointed out Gillespie's skill with people of all nationalities and the success of the State Department tours. Jon Hendricks put presidential words to *Salt Peanuts* and Dizzy himself thoroughly enjoyed the whole operation.

In fact, Gillespie did have his tongue in his cheek. He postulated a change of colour for the White House, suggested Bo Diddley as secretary of state and told doubters that he was running for president because 'We need one'. Nevertheless, by the early part of 1964, there was quite a sizeable support for the new candidate. Gleason's wife Jeannie became something of a campaign manager, and she reported that there was support for Dizzy in more than twenty states. A petition was launched to get John Birks Gillespie placed as an independent candidate for the nation's top post, and a speech was prepared to put over his policies.

Gillespie explained that, on winning the election, he would reside in the Blues House, that income tax would be abolished and that the numbers game would be legalized. To save money, the FBI would be disbanded and all attorneys and judges in the South would be black to even up the score. In addition to this, the Army and Navy would be combined so no promoter could take too big a cut off the top of the double-gig set-up. All ambassadors, except Chester Bowles would be replaced by musicians because they know where it's at. Miles Davis would head up the CIA, Max Roach would be minister of defense and Charles Mingus would be minister of peace. Duke Ellington was to be minister of state, Peggy Lee mistress of labour and so the list went on.

As history shows, Gillespie was not elected to the presidency and in fact failed to get the Californian nomination. He did, however, have a great deal of fun in his token defeat and got some valuable publicity along the way.

This was also a year in which he made two films with John and Faith Hubley. John was a former Walt Disney man, and he and his wife Faith were masters of animation. In *The Hat*, the parts were

Dizzy Gillespie with James Moody and Max Roach

spoken by Gillespie and actor-pianist Dudley Moore, and Dizzy improvised the music. The theme was the futility of geographical as well as racial barriers, but it had a happy resolution as the two protagonists walk into the sunset together.

In *The Hole*, actor George Matthews and Gillespie were the voices grafted onto the black and white characters in a discussion beneath street level. The subject was a possible holocaust, and the film ended with a condemnation of the acquisitive society. Particularly well received by the public, it actually won an Academy Award as the best animated short film of 1963.

Musically, this was also a good time for Gillespie. The quintet with Moody and Barron had stabilized and Dizzy himself was playing extremely well. His contract with Philips Records was working out satisfactorily and he had time to plan his recording dates with care. The marketing took on a more calm attitude, and the 'silly' album titles of the fifties were put behind him.

James Moody proved to be an ideal partner. Born in Savannah, Georgia, he had led his own band in the fifties, playing in a romantic ballad style related, albeit distantly, to Earl Bostic's rhapsodic manner. His single *I'm in the Mood for Love* was a hit, but after a short sabbatical in 1958 he had returned to jazz, stripped of any commercial concessions; playing much as he had with Gillespie in the forties. He had also developed his flute playing to such an extent that he began to feature heavily in critical polls. With the quintet he was featured mainly on tenor, but the tone he achieved on flute fitted well in unison with the muted trumpet in theme statements, and it was also useful as a solo voice.

Kenny Barron also flourished in the band. He came from the flinty Philadelphia school and matched his flowing treble improvisations with an assured grasp of harmonic signposting. Not surprisingly, he was heard at his best on *Cool World*, a film score written by another pianist, Mal Waldron, and recorded by the quintet in April 1964. Originally, the film company had wanted the quintet to play the actual soundtrack, but Gillespie had declined, saying that he would rather do the music in the controlled atmosphere of the recording studio. Happily, the record was a complete success, although Dizzy has always maintained that it bore little resemblance to the film.

Later in '64 he moved over to the Limelight label. There he made an inauspicious start. His first three-day recording project produced music that was hardly memorable. The theme was Caribbean, and West Indian accents were adopted by Gillespie, Moody, bassist Chris White and drummer Kansas Field. Even the instrumental parts were unspectacular, and the whole project seemed to surrender to the novelty elements.

Fortunately, the quintet was still very much intact on the world stage. They played to good notices at the 1965 Newport and Monterey festivals and, at the latter, Gillespie had the opportunity to show that he could be an excellent master of ceremonies. The disasters of his previous experience behind him, he was both charming and amusing and, in addition to his own involvement in the Monterey's fine History of the Trumpets theme, kept the

Dizzy at the Monterey Jazz festival

festival moving along smoothly.

The jazz world in general was in considerable turmoil in the sixties. Bobby Timmons had joined the Art Blakey Jazz Messengers in 1960, and compositions such as *Dat Dere* and *Moanin*, ushered in a movement that quickly acquired the title *soul jazz*. In effect it was a return to the roots, it derived its rhythmic stance from the Baptist rock of Negro church music but used the more sophisticated instrumental techniques of the sixties to weld older blues elements onto the more extended and loose limbed form of bebop that became known as hard bop. The Adderley Brothers picked up on the lead and, by the middle of the sixties,

88

*Dizzy with Don Ellis,
Monterey*

there were a large number of groups flavouring their music with soul spice.

In parallel, the free-form movement had reached second-generation stage. Ornette Coleman had ushered in the free melodic-association music of the late fifties, but the sixties had seen establishment figures like John Coltrane and Sonny Rollins extending jazz into freer areas. The mid-sixties had seen the emergence of men like Archie Shepp, Roswell Rudd, Bill Dixon, Pharoah Sanders and Albert Ayler, yet the distance between the two extremes, typified by Coleman on one hand and Coltrane and Miles Davis on the other, was not as far as it first appeared.

Both retained a strong link with the blues and, although approaching it in totally different ways, both schools regarded improvisation as their *raison d'être*. Gillespie, for his part, remained mainly on the fence. His own stylistic stance was secure and initially he saw little advantage in accommodating either of these musical movements, particularly as both had been sired by discoveries he himself had made twenty years earlier.

There was, however, the nagging feeling that he should make some kind of statement in one or both of the styles. Although, in fact, he was never to become involved with free form, over the next twenty years, he was occasionally persuaded to involve himself in the soul or later rock-fusion movements, usually with rather disappointing results. This was the case in 1966 when he produced a record alternatively entitled *Sweet Soul* and *Souled Out* but the extent of its failure gave an early insight into the incompatibility of his incisive yet multi-detailed melody lines and the rumblingly bluesy backgrounds of soul. Programme director Billy Taylor certainly did not share that view, and he tried just about everything to make the project work. For some titles he introduced a gospel choir, and Gillespie responded with some of the most suspect intonation of his entire career. He also offered *Chicken Giblets*, an attempt at the then popular 'soul march'. On this title, Dizzy actually tried to adjust his phrase shapes to suit the alien form, but again sounded uneasy.

Taylor even tried giving the full pop studio production treatment to some items, but only on the more restrained *Blue Cuchifrito* did Gillespie play anywhere near well, and even then the piece was resolved – by a fadeout. The low spot of the album was *Rutabaga Pie*, a title that persuaded Taylor to describe Gillespie in his sleeve notes as 'powerful and truculent' when what he really meant was diffident, confused and lacking in any sort of belief in the music.

Unfortunately, it was a path that Dizzy was again to tread and, for a short time, it did appear that the Gillespie jazz train had gone off the rails. At the end of 1965, he and his group toured Britain as the warm-up band at organist Jimmy Smith's concerts, a ludicrous case of role reversals. Smith had, by this stage, reached the worst type of formula performance. It may have paraded the 'in vogue' soul accents, but it was an act that had become contrived. To hear Gillespie producing involved versions of favourites like *I Can't Get Started* and *'Round Midnight*, merely to prepare the audience for an organ barrage, was palpably sad.

Almost as if to prove that this state of affairs should be seen as temporary, Gillespie was back in Europe at the end of 1966, this time with the full JATP package and playing impressively. Steve Voce, reporting an English concert at Liverpool (*Jazz Journal*,

Dizzy Gillespie with critic
Max Jones

January 1967), told of his playing brilliant trumpet-tenor
saxophone duets backstage with Coleman Hawkins, 'the parts
coming from a violin concerto which they had memorized'. On
stage, Gillespie had an ally from his own corner in Moody, as well
as his friends and rival Clark Terry to challenge his trumpet
supremacy. The outcome was a tight festival performance blessed
with apposite pyrotechnics as well as thoughtful solo moments.

Strangely enough, it was another off-stage incident that threw
into sharp relief his lack of sympathy for the 'return to the roots'
soul movement. In the artists' bar at London's Royal Festival Hall,
an excited Gillespie interrupted a four-or-five way conversation
involving Clark Terry, *Jazz Journal*'s late founder Sinclair Traill,
and this writer. He insisted that the assembled party return to the
side of the stage because the great T-Bone Walker was in full flight.
Gillespie may have found the anachronistic elements in sixties soul
a trifle unpalatable, but he had no such complaint about the real
thing and proceeded to eulogize at length about the remarkable T-
Bone.

Perhaps one concession that Gillespie made to the fashion of the day was to employ a fender-bass player, and one was in use when he took part in the Puebla Festival in early 1967. This event in Mexico, sponsored by American Airlines celebrating its twenty-fifth anniversary, presented an abbreviated version of the Newport Jazz Festival. Audience response at the festival was good, Gillespie topped the bill on the main night, and the Auditorio de la Reforma was packed to standing room. The trumpeter wooed his new fans with the inevitable *Manteca* and *Con Alma*, but Stanley Dance reported that a restrained *Morning of the Carnival* received equal acclaim (*Jazz Journal*, July 1967).

Fender-player Russell George was also in action at the Monterey Festival later in the year, but performances did place question marks against the wisdom of the choice. Since Gillespie was comprising in no other way, there seemed little reason to saddle the rhythm section with a stolid, more pronounced pulse. Gillespie's rhythm teams had usually enjoyed the advantage of at least one extra percussionist and had achieved a relaxed, floating flexibility as a result. To take one aspect of the soul style, and at that the least attractive, could do very little for his music unless he was prepared to adapt completely.

In retrospect, it was the very uncertain nature of the jazz world that was the problem. Moody was still a pillar of strength in the touring band, and Gillespie had just recruited the talented pianist Mike Longo. Dizzy still worked with certain JATP packages and was a welcome guest at most of the world's top festivals. He did not, however, have a long term recording contract and issued only two orthodox small-group records as a leader between 1967 and 1971.

Both were on location recordings, but one, played at a Village Vanguard Sunday Brunch with violinist-trumpeter Ray Nance, underlined Dizzy's suspicion of soul and his continued allegiance to loosely shifting backgrounds. His line-up included pianist Chick Corea, bassist Richard Davis and drummer Mel Lewis, and their music made no use of exotic soul decoration. The inclusion of drummer Elvin Jones for one number proposed a different situation, however, for it presented Gillespie with the doyen of the implied accent and the swirlingly rhythmic under-tow. Although it must be said that Jones tempered his style to suit the occasion, there was enough interaction with Gillespie to suggest that both parties found it stimulating.

Fortunately, most of Dizzy's musical stimulation in 1968 came from big-band work. In July he was invited to form an orchestra for the Newport Festival. Gil Fuller conducted, and there were new arrangements from him and also from Benny Carter. The band sported two drummers in Candy Finch and Art Blakey, and the crowd responded as was appropriate, although reports were that

Dizzy Gillespie

the solo work was better than the occasionally untidy ensembles.

The band was dubbed the 20th Anniversary Reunion Big Band and, with minor changes in personnel, it set off on a European tour. By the time it shared the bill with the Mike Westbook Band at London's Hammersmith Odeon, trumpeter Benny Bailey and tenor saxophonist Harold Land had been replaced, but the ensemble was now in better order. It reflects no criticism of Mike Westbrook, but it must be said that at Jazz 'Expo 68' there was insufficient time for Gillespie, in a shared programme presented in two houses per evening. Nevertheless, Gillespie was at his effusive

93

best, and there were impressive contributions from Moody and from trombonists Curtis Fuller and Tom McIntosh. The highlight of the concert was a Jimmy Owens' composition called *Milan Is Love*. With its delightful theme, it brought the young flugelhorn player into a friendly duel with his leader – with superb results.

The band had rehearsed in New York for five days, but when the need to graft in two European players occurred, they had available only one day at Ronnie Scott's Club in London. The tour included Belgium, Denmark, Finland, France, Italy and Sweden, but the band did improve 'on the hoof', and by the time it reached the Berlin Philharmonic Hall in Germany, the leader told Joachim Berendt that he would be hearing 'my best band since 1948'.

Fortunately, the concert was recorded, and the resulting issue did nothing to discredit that opinion. The section work was a model of precision, with the trumpets especially notable. There were more outstanding solos from Moody, Owens and the leader, stylish new arrangements from Longo, and a feeling of good humour permeating the whole event. Gillespie was delighted, particularly as the audiences at Berlin's futuristic hall have a reputation for being hard to please. In this case, they were ecstatic and, in fact, many hundreds remained at the end to hear extra takes that were required for the planned record.

Returning home was actually an emotional let down for Gillespie. Somehow this time it seemed even harder. On 4 April 1968, Dr. Martin Luther King Jr., the man of peace, was murdered on the balcony of a Memphis motel. The man whose intellectual affinity with India's Mahatma Gandhi had led him to make the famous pacifist statement 'We will not hate you, but we will not obey your evil laws' was dead.

With his passing many looked to Robert F. Kennedy as the leader trusted by all races. His political star was on the ascendency, but on 5 June, he was murdered in a hotel in Los Angeles. These tragedies greatly saddened the American nation, but it was King's death that had the greater effect on Gillespie. His immediate reaction on the day of the murder was to get extremely drunk, as if to shut out the horror.

Drinking had always been something of a refuge for him in times of stress. He was aware of the short-term hazards, as well as the threat to his long-time health, but psychologically it was good for him. The biggest problem in the short term was that it made him somewhat anti-social and, more important, it impaired his playing. He had endured one dreadful experience on a Japanese tour when, together with many members of the band, he had misjudged the potency of sake.

This, perhaps as much as anything else, had made him susceptible to anything that might suggest giving up drink. In the

Dizzy Gillespie's quintet: Mike Longo (piano), Al Gafa (guitar), Alex Blake (double bass), Dizzy (trumpet) and Mickey Roker (drums)

event, it came about through religion. While in Milwaukee, Gillespie was approached by a woman interested in discussing his music and his artistic relationship with Charlie Parker. On the surface, she seemed genuine and, after initial refusal, Gillespie agreed to meet her. They spoke together for some time about Dizzy's early life, about his family, but only a limited amount about the Bird.

It was to be the first of several meetings with the woman and her husband, and it turned out that she was involved in the Baha'i faith. Gillespie became extremely interested, and the woman, Beth McKintey, arranged for pamphlets to be sent to him. In many ways, it was like preaching to the converted. Like Gillespie himself, the Baha'i centred on the oneness of all mankind and proclaimed that there should be no suggestion of a superior race. Baha'is were champions of world unity and held that peace was the all-important human state. For Gillespie there was one minor barrier. As he had discovered with the McKinteys, Baha'is did not drink alcohol.

Dizzy Gillespie and Mary Lou Williams

Suddenly this seemed a very small barrier. Gillespie decided to stop drinking and to become fully committed to the faith. As with all major steps that he has taken in his life, this was not done in a half-hearted way. He began to read prolifically and to go back to the ultimate source of the religion. Baha' Ullah had been a mid-19th century Persian prophet, who disapproved of religious diversification and had felt that Moses, Krishna, Jesus and Muhammad really aspired to the same ideals. For an intelligent man like Gillespie, whose life had often been torn by futile racial differences, Baha'i had much to offer.

Musically, he was not as settled. In the fall of 1969, he recorded a set made up mainly of the better pop tunes of the day. The arranging and conducting were done by Don Sebesky, and the group was driven by Pretty Purdie's powerful rock drumming. The set was not altogether successful, however, and the obvious conclusion was again that Gillespie's playing found its best expression with material designed for it.

This theory was further supported shortly thereafter when Dizzy made another abortive attempt to cash in on the soul craze. A fine band as overlaid with a barrage of guitarists and percussionists and with a female choir to add the final touches.

96

It must be noted that it was earlier in that same year, 1969, that Miles Davis had recorded his highly influential *In a Silent Way* and *Bitches Brew*. Davis had gone on record as saying that he had not been reaching his own people, and his using of basic rhythm and blues principles was his way of redressing the balance. Although he later took his band's style nearer to the field of white rock, he had set the house rules for the trumpet-led jazz-rock unit.

Characteristically, Gillespie made no attempt to follow the same route. Flirting with soul jazz had been one thing, but surrendering the trumpet's pre-eminent position to a multi-rhythmed instrumental choir was something else. Gillespie had never aspired to Davis's kind of smouldering intensity. Even his most heartfelt moments had a clear cut legibility – a way of telling a moving story intelligibly for the lay listener but with enough rhetoric to impress students of a trumpet-playing art.

The 1970 Newport Festival underlined this position, and it also provided a timely reminder of Gillespie's status in the hierarchy of the instrument. Producer George Wein set aside one evening as a 70th birthday salute to Louis Armstrong. The great man was not in good health, but he made an enthusiastic appearance and sang some of his favourite numbers. He left the trumpet team of Wild Bill Davison, Dizzy Gillespie, Bobby Hackett, Ray Nance, Joe Newman and Jimmy Owens to pay their own individual tributes, and each played a number associated with the Satchmo legend.

Gillespie seemed visibly moved and described Louis Armstrong's stature in the history of jazz as 'unimpeachable' and, to the amusement of the audience, thanked him for making the Gillespie livelihood possible. The evening ended with Armstrong leading the singing of *The Saints* and the musicians parading around the Festival Field. One year later he was dead.

The days when the trumpet crown was passed on to the obvious successor had long passed into the mists of legend, but there was no doubting the fact that Gillespie remained one of the genuine Armstrong disciples, whatever the distance from the source. Dizzy was not immune to the music of the sixties, however, and when Moody left the group in 1969, his replacement was guitarist George Davis. It was a gesture that acknowledged the overall music scene, but it did not change the group's commitment to jazz, devoid of extraneous trappings. Guitarist Al Gafa replaced Davis in 1971, and in the same year hard-hitting drummer Mickey Roker joined the band for what turned out to be an eight-year stay.

Gillespie undertook sessions of any kind in 1970 and 1971, and then mainly on location and not with his regular group. Despite this, they tended to be musically productive and often placed him in challenging situations. At the Overseas Press Club in New York in early 1971, he was teamed with Dixieland trumpeter Bobby

Hackett and with a virtual swing-era rhythm section made up of pianist Mary Lou Williams, bassist George Duvivier and drummer Grady Tate. It looked like a formula for failure, but years of JATP touring had taught Gillespie how to accommodate vastly different styles, and his duels with the lyrical Rhode Island trumpeter were a delight.

In complete contrast, 1971 saw the formation of a group that teamed Gillespie with five men who ate, slept and breathed the same music. The sextet was completed by saxophonist Sonny Stitt, trombonist Kai Winding, Thelonious Monk, bassist Al McKibbon, and Art Blakey, and not without some justification they called themselves the Giants of Jazz. Their first British concert was at London's Victoria Cinema toward the end of the year and it proved to be a triumph for all concerned. From the moment that the sounds of *Blue 'N' Boogie* echoed through the old art-deco cinema, raw bebop was on show.

Monk and Stitt played well, and the rhythm section was imaginative and supple, but for all their outstanding efforts it was Gillespie who stole the show. Amongst some notes made by this writer on the night, attention was drawn to a superb bass-trumpet duo on *Tin Tin Deo*, a darkly moody *'Round Midnight*, and a wonderfully frenetic *Wee*. One was not aware of listening to jazz that belonged stylistically twenty five years earlier. It came over as a totally contemporaneous experience, as if bebop was being performed for the first time.

Most American jazz fans were pleased to see 1971 come to a close. It was the year when the yobs and bullies, aptly described by critic Ira Gitler as the lost tribes of the Woodstock Nation, had done their best to destroy the Newport Jazz Festival. They had broken up camp chairs, rendered a piano irreparable, virtually demolished the stage and generally desecrated the whole image of the event.

Fortunately, promoter George Wein was more resilient than the hooligan element had anticipated, and the Newport Jazz Festival – New York rose phoenix-like from the cultural pyre that had engulfed the Rhode Island disaster. The formula was different, but it was so effective that it was to become the pattern of performance until the present time (1988). Concerts were presented at the Philharmonic Hall (later renamed Avery Fisher) and Carnegie Hall and patrons were encouraged to ferry between the two venues. Ancillary-performance areas and clubs, putting on their festival face, contributed and the festival became a totally urban phenomenon.

The 1972 event was more successful than Wein had dared to hope and media response was tremendous. Local radio stations introduced special jazz slots, the *Daily News* ran superb

The Giants of Jazz: Kai
Winding (trombone), Dizzy
Gillespie (trumpet), Al
McKibbon (double bass),
Sonny Stitt (tenor
saxophone) and Art Blakey
(drums)

photographic coverage and the *Times* reviewed every major event
in detail. There were seminars in Lincoln Center, riverboat
shuffles up the Hudson River and, perhaps the highlight of the 1972
event, two massive jam sessions at Radio City Music Hall.

On the nights in question, there were queues on three sides of
the big old cinema and attendances exceeded 6,000 for each. Jazz
fans came to see, amongst others, Dizzy Gillespie doing battle with
Stan Getz, trombonist Bennie Green and Milt Jackson. The
rhythm section for the event was made up of Mary Lou Williams,
bassist Percy Heath, Max Roach and Georgia conga specialist Big

Black. Critical opinion was unanimously that the jam-session idea was ideal for both the venue and the circumstances and that Gillespie, ripping through items like *Bag's Groove* and his beloved *Tunisia*, was in superb lip.

In some way his success tied in with his resurgent political aspirations and in 1972 Gillespie again decided to run for president. Eventually he backed down, but he made it clear that he had not planned to stand as 'a criticism of the actions of anyone who holds or aspires to this high position of government'. All that he wanted to do was to 'bring together the peoples of the world in unity so that all wars may cease'.

The Giants of Jazz were back in Europe toward the end of the year, but the relaxed and optimistic air of 1971 appeared to be

Dizzy Gillespie with Al McKibbon

Dizzy Gillespie with George Weir

missing. There were troubles with the P.A. at London's New Victoria Cinema, Monk seemed at his most truculent and unapproachable, while McKibbon was beset by all kinds of electrical problems on his own amplification. Gillespie and Stitt played well, but it appeared to be a group on the point of dissolution. So it was to prove, Monk's health had deteriorated, and the Giants sadly decided to disband. It had been a worthwhile exercise, since many people had heard bebop in its original form for the first time. Two live sessions had been recorded, but the band had run its course, and to have progressed beyond this point, possibly without Monk, would have been self-defeating.

Gillespie was in Europe without the group in 1973, but it was an occurrence at home that nearly brought him to ultimate defeat. He had been on the wagon for some time but, while working in New York's Village Vanguard, was offered some kind of stimulant. Unwisely, he accepted, and within a very short time collapsed on stage. The set was abandoned, the audience cleared from the club

101

Dizzy Gillespie with Tony Scott and Max Roach

and, with the help of a friend, Mike Longo got him outside – for some fresh air.

To avoid publicity, it was decided not to take him to hospital. A neighbour of Gillespie's was still around and he drove him home. It certainly seemed a sensible solution and an extremely worried Lorraine put her half-conscious husband straight to bed. Fortunately, her concern made her extra-diligent and, when checking on him shortly after, she found him 'frothing at the mouth and having convulsions'. She rushed him to hospital where he was received officially Dead-On-Arrival!

The doctors and nurses at the hospital were not ready for any such premature exit, however, and by their prompt and expert actions, they returned John Birks Gillespie to the land of the living. For the trumpeter it was a salutary experience, one that he swore would never be repeated. His life within the Baha'i faith had already made him more conservative in his attitudes. He determined to make that state of mind even more positive. He had perhaps taken Lorraine for granted, and he resolved that this would never be the case again.

102

CHAPTER 9

BLUES FOR NORMAN

Richard Nixon had become president in 1968 but by 1973 the Watergate scandal had involved his administration in a web of deceit and duplicity. In contrast, Gillespie's return to the world of the living started a period of his life that was to be emotionally satisfying as well as musically fulfilling.

The Kenyan government, celebrating ten years of independence, made him a guest of honour at the festivities. He was particularly gratified by this and determined to respond in an appropriate manner. Naturally he was expected to play, but he also went to the trouble of writing a suitable speech, having it translated at the embassy in Washington, and delivering it – in Swahili.

Musically, he got a comparable lift, one that was to give him a much welcomed sense of security. His former confrère Norman Granz, after selling his Verve label in 1961, had moved to Geneva and, although returning to America for a JATP tour in 1967, had declared that this would be the last such tour and that he had decided to stay mainly in Europe.

He had, however, missed the hurly-burly of the music industry and, with his contractual limitation long since expired, he decided to return to the record business. The Pablo label was born in 1973 and its producer was demonstrating all his old enthusiasms. Predictably, its stylistic stance was an extension of the Verve ideal. Twelve years on, it was not about to embrace free form music or, in fact, any other form of jazz with which Granz might not feel comfortable. The artists recorded were, in the main, men with either JATP backgrounds or, at least, similar musical predilections. Granz's thoroughbred friend Gillespie was an obvious choice for the stable, and on 19 September 1974 he made his Pablo debut in the company of Joe Pass.

Working for Pablo set Dizzy a wide variety of musical challenges, each setting its own unique type of problem. On this

Dizzy with Clark Terry and Harry Edison

first session he had from Pass the kind of light, punchy background that demanded a buoyancy of expression. Up-tempo items tended to take the battle directly to Pass but, with Ben Brown and Mickey Roker in the rhythm section, the guitarist did very much more than cope. The upshot was that Gillespie's spitting, rapid-fire arpeggios found their match in the figures of a player articulate at even the most crippling speeds.

A completely different set of rules was to pertain on his next session, made in the company of fellow-trumpeters Roy Eldridge, Clark Terry and Harry Edison. Their task was to back the explosive voice of Joe Turner and, although it tested each player's powers as a bluesman, it put little pressure on their subtlety. The results were surprisingly good, but for Gillespie it represented just another session before again donning his globe-trotting shoes.

Once again he went to Europe, and for the 1974 trip he took his

104

own quartet with Al Gafa, Mickey Roker and bassist Earl May. One special event on the trip was the Portuguese Cascais Festival, sponsored by the local government's travel and cultural authorities. The theme of the festival was the *Musical Life of Charlie Parker* and, in addition to playing in his own group, Gillespie also joined Red Rodney, Sonny Stitt, Lockjaw Davis, Budd Johnson and Bobby Tucker in a group that had been dubbed, not inappropriately, the Bop All Stars.

For Gillespie the next port of call was England and a three week residency at Ronnie Scott's Club in London. This writer was present on at least three occasions, and it was a situation that offered a chance to hear Dizzy, with a suitcase unpacked and his braces metaphorically down.

Fortunately, it was not one that revealed the deity with feet of clay. It did, however, make clear that one must not be idealistic about the creative process. In a protracted club residency it was inevitable that Gillespie would coast in a way that he would find neither necessary nor tactical in a shorter concert engagement. He was now fifty-eight and he had certainly lost some of his zest for involvement at the mind-stretching level.

For perhaps the first time, one was aware of the master trumpeter really guarding his 'chops'. He sang in his brilliantly boppish way, he played piano and, although he beat his own unique tattoo on the congas, his trumpet was to his lips only when necessary. Strangely enough, this economy of expression seemed to heighten the listener's awareness of the man's superbly natural feeling for jazz. It was when he took off on short but highly personal journeys that, for several choruses, the audience became intensely aware of the man's inspirational genius. It did not matter if it was *Con Alma*, *Monteca* or *Tunisia* – here was a genuine original playing jazz in a way that cannot be taught.

In January 1975, Gillespie again showed that he was the master of one type of fusion – the coming together of South and North American music. At New York's St. Patrick's Cathedral on Fifth Avenue he played a concert with the Machito Orchestra and marked up a stunning success. Machito was born Frank Grillo in Tampa, Florida, had been raised in Cuba and had spent much of his musical life there. At various times he had employed Charlie Parker, Flip Phillips, Howard McGhee and Johnny Griffin, and, although hardly a jazzman, he had a great affinity for the music. At St. Patrick's the band included Gillespie's friend from the Calloway days, Mario Bauza, and the two horns basked in the Latin cross-rhythms of the section that had updated its image with electric pianos and synthesizers.

Five months later Granz, very taken with the idea, recreated the concert on record and a studio version was issued. Gillespie was happy and, with Granz back in the driving seat, he had his annual Montreux triumph. He was also part of a superb package that Granz brought to England later in the year. At London's famous Palladium he showed himself more than willing to pit his musical wits against Terry and Eldridge even if, behind the scenes, the Dizzy behaviour had become more decorous. Steve Voce (*Jazz Journal*, November 1975), who travelled briefly with the band, reported that Gillespie was still in good joke-telling form but that he had announced to guests in his hotel lobby that 'These other guys have been trying to tear Europe apart all at once. I've been behaving myself.' How deeply his tongue was embedded into his cheek is not known, but Gillespie was taking care of business – and himself.

Whatever his own feelings, there is no doubt that the establishment had begun to think of him as one of jazz's elder statesmen. The impact of the State Department tours was still being felt and, although some government officials were wary, Gillespie had friends in high places. In 1976, he was asked to appear on the floor of the State House in his home state, South Carolina. He was asked not only to play trumpet but also to make a speech that would become a permanent entry in records of the Sovereign State of Carolina. He was immensely flattered, but he did not take a soft option. He chose as the basis for his address an article from a Baha'i journal '200 Years of Imperishable Hope'.

It was principally about American history and, although it accepted the premise that the country would one day enjoy racial harmony, it did not ignore the horrors of the past. Gillespie called on his own experience and drew special attention to the fact that the prejudice of the South differed greatly from that of the North. He felt that integrated education had perhaps advanced more in the South and cited the three schools in his home town of Cheraw and the way in which all pupils got on. With his usual impish sense of humour, he could not resist a mention of the low-rent housing on Dizzy Gillespie Drive, a street named in his honour – and he thought an object lesson to the North.

Further recognition came at national level, when he was asked to join the 'jazz and folk' section of the National Endowment for the Arts. This gave him another opportunity to gallop one of his favourite hobbyhorses, and, before accepting, he drew attention to the fact that jazz, the country's 'only indigenous music', was scheduled to receive just a fraction of the $13,000,000 allocated to the music programme in the following year. Gillespie felt that the reason that jazz was downgraded was that it would have challenged an important racial issue. He said that 'to put jazz on the plane that it deserves would mean elevating the creators of our music, who happen to be black – to put them on a level above the music of the

Dizzy Gillespie

white citizenry'. The point was well made.

Perhaps more than any other working musician, Gillespie began to show that he had completely overcome jazz's old inferiority complex. He was not prepared to apologize for any aspect of his craft and saw its adaptability as its strength. Music that could be classified as truly contemporary and could embrace night-club entertainment, art music, descriptive music for the visual arts, or be just plain dance music had a great deal to recommend it.

In fact, in 1976 he devoted his only studio recording date as a leader to the production of what he called a dance album. Unfortunately, a record that confirmed jazz's continued viability as a dance music did not find in Gillespie the best ambassador of the fact. It made inappropriate rhythmic concessions and, more significantly, it found the trumpeter himself prepared either to surrender his own 'sound of surprise' to the production of predictable and danceable phrase shapes or to play his deliciously boppish runs straight over the shuffling boogaloo rhythms, ignoring their rhythmic intentions. Neither alternative was appropriate, and the suggestion could once again be made, not that he was going commercial, but that he was trying to go young.

Another session given the youthful treatment came early in the following year, this time with a mammoth production 'team' led by his former colleague Lalo Shifrin. On its own terms it was a success, and one of the recorded titles, *Unicorn*, became a minor hit. It certainly posed the question, Could it be that the cult of youth was closing in – even on Gillespie?

The answer came from an unexpected source and it had special implications. A young Californian, Jon Faddis, emerged as a devout Gillespie disciple. Born in 1953, he had become acquainted with his hero's music at the age of nine. By the time he reached eleven, he had discovered a trumpet teacher, Bill Catalano, who was able to instruct in the art of playing Dizzy style. He first met his ultimate mentor at the Monterey Jazz Festival in 1968, accosting him to autograph *fifty* of his records. Gillespie signed every one

and, some weeks later, invited the teenager with the flamboyant Afro hairstyle to sit in with him at the Jazz Workshop in San Francisco. Faddis told Martin Richards (*Jazz Journal International*, 1986) 'He got me up on stage and we played Jimmy Owens' tune *Get That Moody Blues* and *Satin Doll*. I almost fainted I was so nervous. I started shaking and the room started spinning, but I was playing with Dizzy.'

Following this experience, Faddis set about mastering the impossibly difficult Gillespie style in earnest, making no secret of the fact that he regarded this as his most effective route to instrumental mastery. His reputation grew quickly and he came to the attention of the whole jazz world in the Thad Jones-Mel Lewis Big Band in the early seventies. As early as 1974 he sat in with his mentor in New York clubs, but it was in 1977 that they made their first recording together. Inevitably, this was a great thrill for the twenty-four-year-old Oakland player, but its significance was not lost on Gillespie.

Here was a young man superbly equipped as a trumpeter and interested only in playing bebop and, most particularly, Gillespie's brand of bebop. Throughout his life Gillespie had been a major influence on his instrument. His inspiration to Fats Navarro, Miles Davis, Clifford Brown, Lee Morgan, Freddie Hubbard, Don Cherry and Lester Bowie had been immeasurable and it would be impossible to think of a major trumpeter not touched by his genius. Yet Gillespie had been under siege to pander to young, immature musical tastes, not by seeking new horizons in his own jazz ethic, but by playing music that remained alien to him.

Faddis was a gifted musician and he was reversing that process. He was young but he was reminding Gillespie that real music was timeless. Their joint recording was, in fact, made live at Montreux, and it came about despite a massive breakdown in communications. The two trumpeters had landed as scheduled in Switzerland, while their luggage – in this case a rhythm section including Rodney Jones, Ben Brown and Mickey Roker – had ended up in Holland. With plans to record the live performance already under way, a patchwork contingency plan was put into service. Milt Jackson, pianist Monty Alexander, drummer Jimmie Smith, and Ray Brown were hurredly recruited and an under-rehearsed band went on stage.

The outcome was highly successful, and critic Alun Morgan was tempted (*Jazz Journal International*, 1977) to compare the two-trumpet team to the Gillespie–Eldridge situation of twenty years earlier. His astute observation was supported by the recorded evidence and, although in his sleeve note Granz suggested that listeners might experience difficulty in telling the two players apart, his fears proved groundless. While there was no doubt that Faddis had borrowed the basis of the older man's style, he had already begun to stamp his own personality on it. It was a situation that put Gillespie on his mettle and seemed to make him determined to concede nothing to his protégé.

If any further proof that the 1977 Gillespie saw no lasting need to 'go young' was needed, it was found in the evidence provided by his touring band. Typical was his annual pilgrimage to Ronnie Scott's in London, where he again used his normal line-up, including Jones, Brown and Roker, and played orthodox sets. More was heard of his 'locked-hands' piano style, as well as of his superbly rhythmic singing, and although he introduced a novel 'preaching' coda to *Night in Tunisia*, he played straight-ahead trumpet with only a little exotica on the side.

In November 1977 Gillespie played at the White House for President Jimmy Carter, with Sarah Vaughan and Earl Hines. Carter was yet another president who took a middle line on racism. He was prepared to uphold rights already established but showed few signs of moving appreciably further. On the debit side, he did little to acknowledge the employment problems of black youth and did virtually nothing to arrest the decay of black neighbourhoods.

He did, however, prove to be susceptible to the charm of Gillespie, and during their White House meeting he expressed his enthusiasm for jazz. He actually went further and joined the long list of American dignitaries who have claimed that they would elevate jazz to the social and artistic level of classical music.

Unlike many, however, Carter did begin to give jazz presidential approbation. In June 1978, he hosted a White House Jazz Festival to celebrate the 25th anniversary of the Newport Jazz Festival. He invited thirty performing musicians and a large number of critics, politicians, musicians and show business celebrities. In his *Jazz Journal International* report (September 1978) Lee Jeske quoted Carter as saying, 'If there ever was an indigenous art form, one that was special and peculiar to the United States, representing what we are as a country, I would say that it was jazz.'

Gillespie played a superb set in the company of Dexter Gordon, Herbie Hancock and George Benson, but it was the finale that crowned the day. Asked by the president if he would close the show, Gillespie played a duet with a Max Roach, armed only with his high-hat drum. Then, to cap it all, the audacioius Dizzy man grabbed the mike and announced, 'Now the president . . . his highness, has asked us to play one more number, *Salt Peanuts*; but there are strings attached. The president himself . . . his majesty, sire, is going to sing the lyrics.' Smiling his famous smile, Jimmy Carter joined Dizzy and became the first holder of America's highest office to perform as a bop singer.

The year 1978 saw Gillespie at most of the festivals, but it also

had him moving into the commercial world and endorsing a most unlikely product. 'Dizzy Digs LP' was the slogan devised to advertise conga and bongo drums, and the resulting poster showed Gillespie leaning on three drums, glasses off, and with his trumpet up-turned on the skins. Whether the advertisement sold more congas for Latin Percussion is not known, but it did expose the trumpeter to a lot of good-natured banter from his fellow musicians.

It was also a year that saw the completion of another enterprise. Much of Gillespie's time had been taken up, together with Al Fraser, in finalising the book *To Be or Not to Bop*. The project had been undertaken five years earlier and it had originally aspired to the lofty ideal of 'creating the best – the most authentic and authoritative autobiography of a jazz musician ever published'. Although falling short of such a goal, it appeared, first published by Doubleday in New York in 1979 and by W H Allen in London in 1980, as a highly colourful if contentious account of this remarkable player's life and music.

Gillespie's good friend Charles Mingus died in January 1979, and the trumpeter played a prominent part in a Village Gate 'Salute to Mingus' event. Later in the year, he played an extraordinary concert at Carnegie Hall as part of the Newport–New York Festival. It was entitled 'Unity with Diversity' and featured Gillespie alone with nine percussionists. The impressive line-up included Grady Tate, Jo Jones, J. C. Heard, Roy Haynes, Art Blakey, Bernard Purdie, Tito Puente, Luis Peralta and Carlos 'Palato' Valdes. Max Roach and Michael Carvin joined in, to bring the roster up to eleven, and Gillespie bubbled freely over the top. The sound level was inevitably thunderous and for two and a half hours the trumpeter did just what he wanted. The whole exercise was most successful and he ended the evening dancing in the aisle.

Fifty years after the birth of Charlie Parker, London's Capitol Radio staged a 'Year of the Bird' concert in the Royal Festival Hall during 1980. The Brecker Brothers showed that there were modern ways of reading the altoist's doctrine, but it was still Gillespie's masterful *Yardbird Suite* that climaxed the evening. For the rest of the year it was festivals as normal, as indeed it was for 1981, as well.

That year, however, saw the beginning of 'Jazz America', an eight million-dollar project to present American television's history of jazz in a series scheduled to take four years. One of the opening events, at New York's Avery Fisher Hall, was dubbed Dizzy Gillespie's Dream Band but also featured a superb sextet with the trumpeter at its head. For the event he was dressed in a purple velvet tuxedo, but it was his crackling trumpet that made the greater impression, and with rivals such as Faddis, Marvin

Stamm and Joe Wilder on hand, it was no easy ride.

Gillespie had always been a man who made friends and kept them. He had always got on well with British club owner Ronnie Scott, and later in 1981 he was delighted to take a spot at the London venue as part of its rather special Autumn Festival. His new quintet, with altoist Paquito Rivera, guitarist Ed Cherry, bassist Mike Howell and drummer Ignacio Berroa, was outstanding but Gillespie was not hiding behind their impressive talents. The material used was hardly a surprise, but there was precious little coasting and one felt that Dizzy was saying a 'thank you' for the years of their professional association.

The endless round of festivals again dominated 1982, and during that year Gillespie celebrated his sixty-fifth birthday. Like most people, age reminded him of the value of his friends. He had lost so many over the years, and being sixty-five seemed to heighten his awareness of them. Even people who had occasionally proved difficult in his life seemed important, and he showed no hesitation in accepting an invitation to take part in the 'Tribute to Buddy Rich' night at New York's Kool Festival, with the volatile drummer in full control. He found himself alongside Harry 'Sweets' Edison, occasionally in conflict with the battling Rich, but, according to eye witnesses, able to use his trumpet as a flag of truce.

Steve Voce (*Jazz Journal International*, September 1982) reported that Gillespie played a memorable *I Remember Clifford* with Art Farmer at the Nice Festival of that year. Although a fine musician, Farmer was hardly likely to be considered as a brother-in-arms in terms of trumpet-playing. Ironically, unlikely associations had suited Gillespie in the past. To meet the challenge he did not change his own trumpet style in any drastic way, but he seemed to adapt to the other player in emotional terms. It was as if, now an older and perhaps wiser man, he was even more able to pitch his own performance within the other player's conceptual range.

The minor adjustment was never merely an emotional muting, and to prove the point he showed how easily he could accommodate the extrovert elements of another's performance. At Britain's 1982 Knebworth Festival, he surprised many listeners by taking on the powerfully modern saxophonist Chico Freeman and by matching singer Bobby McFerrin in a cross-fire of stage front oratory. He also played supremely well with the Crusaders, answering their funk-based questions with a mixture of bop rhetoric and old-world big-band know-how. In each case, it was Gillespie who made the small adjustment of attitude, yet he did so without a hint of compromise or incongruity.

Throughout the eighties, he worked tirelessly, still committed to the festival circuit, and always prepared to be involved in the most varied of musical situations. At the Kool in 1983, he chose Saratoga Springs as the place to play an enchanting duet with Art Blakey. In the same year at Nice he grafted drummer J C Heard into his own group with stunning effect, and on various other occasions revealed himself a compulsive experimentalist.

For a Christmas present in that year he was given a new Schilke trumpet by his friend Jon Faddis. Needless to say, it was a model fitted with an upturned bell but it did make an appreciable difference to his playing. He told critic Mike Hennessey (*Jazz Journal International*, July 1984) that he could not have been more delighted. 'The sound is crisp and round – like bells playing – and I'm surprising myself with what I can do on that horn. Everything I attempt comes off. Guys I know who have heard me play recently ask me what I am doing that is different. But I'm not playing any differently. It's the horn – I can attempt things that I wouldn't have dared to try before.'

The important thing was that it helped to keep the Gillespie spirits buoyant. No challenge was too much, and he was more than comfortable to accept George Wein's invitation to share a night at the 1984 Kool Festival with Sun Ra. Kenny Clarke happened to be in New York at the time, and there was inevitably some speculation as to whether he might appear. In the event, he did not and, perhaps because Gillespie's group featured both the swing style of Benny Carter and the bop of J J Johnson, the drummer used was Louis Bellson.

Present at the concert, this writer was initially surprised to discover that the spectacular Arkestra had been billed to occupy the first half of the programme. It actually turned out to be a wise decision. Sun Ra led his 'space walks', introduced the dances and indulged in all of his intergalactic mumbo-jumbo, but it was Gillespie who by the end of the evening had the blasé New Yorkers in a mild state of shock.

Unfortunately, there were still occasions when Gillespie's judgment in matters musical was erratic. When he had the wherewithal he played in big bands with much of the old fire. With his working group he overcame the limitations that his choice of repertoire placed upon it, but in 1984 he made the worst record he had ever allowed to be issued. Called *Closer to the Source* it was his debut release for the Atlantic label. It employed Stevie Wonder, saxophonists Branford Marsalis and Sonny Fortune, pianist Kenny Kirkland, as well as bassist Marcus Miller and percussionist Mino Cinelu. The formula funk elements of the music were despatched with aplomb by the rhythm section, the sound mix was good, and the traffic of the cross-rhythms was never congested. But, it was Gillespie, not playing well and seemingly unsure of how to respond to the demands of the music, who failed. His note production was less than perfect, and his whole approach was best described as tentative. His previously abortive flirtations with this area of music had taught him little and, in using musicians associated with Miles Davis, he centred attention on his own stylistic incompatability.

His whole position regarding cross-over forms has remained ambivalent. He has never played well as a funk soldier, but the uniform did seem to have a fatal attraction for him. As an internationally feted jazz musician, he had certainly earned the right to express himself in any way he chose but he could not carp if observers pointed out the shortcomings of the outcome.

If, as in the following year, he chose to work with the modest talents of singer Lilian Terry, it was of small consequence. Together they performed for Italy's progressive Soul Note label. The resulting record was pleasing, but the trumpeter could have had few illusions about the critical reaction to such an undemanding piece of music-making.

What was of more significance was his attendance at Cuba's Jazz Latino Plaza International Festival held in Havana in 1985. Originally called merely Jazz Plaza, it had begun in 1979 in a fairly modest way. It had grown, however, and Gillespie's presence in 1985 and again in 1986 was a considerable boost to the local musicians and to the Plaza municipality House of Culture. In some ways, it gave Dizzy a chance to say another 'thank you', this time to the people who had been so important to him in the days of cubop.

In 1987, Gillespie was seventy, an age rarely attained by hard-blowing trumpeters who have consistently worked for most weeks of the year. Predictably, this particular trumpeter was gratified by his three-score-years-and-ten status. In public it took the form of near-euphoria, and one might rightly assume a similar state pertained in his private life.

The jazz world responded accordingly. Gillespie found himself with a big band and a full booking programme. The band, armed with some challenging new arrangements, was very much an all-star unit. Faddis led an impressive trumpet team that also included Virgil Jones and Earl Gardner. The outstanding trombone choir comprised Frank Lacy, Steve Turre and Britt Woodman, and sitting in the reed department were Howard Johnson on baritone and avant garde guru Sam Rivers on tenor. With James Williams making up the strength on piano, the band was not short of quality soloists and, as reports on the European tour showed, Gillespie found this a stimulating situation. Cuban trumpeter Arturo Sandoval guested at the North Sea Festival in The Hague and brought his special high-note talents to a concert tour that honoured the importance of Gillespie's chosen instrument almost as much as it did the man himself.

Much the same occurred in his adopted musical home, New York. At the 1987 JVC Festival a fitting night of tribute opened with the young and gifted trumpeter Wynton Marsalis playing various Dizzy favourites and offering a moving musical bouquet entitled *The Source*. The dedicatee was visibly moved and later fronted the big band to round out an evening in which emotion played almost as large a part in the proceedings as did the music. Ironically, an even more impressive concert took place later in the same week, upstate in Saratoga Springs. Marsalis had sat in during the Carnegie Hall concert, but at the Saratoga Performing Arts Center he joined the band for the entire set.

It was a night to remember. Gillespie, usually in the past an instant creator, seemed strangely diffident at the beginning of the performance. Faddis and Marsalis were in impressive form from the first note, and their mentor willingly gave them centre stage. Inevitably the musical tension grew. Gillespie began to join the musical jousting and to play with daunting authority. The iron-lipped Faddis lanced into the music's rarified upper atmosphere, leaving Gillespie and Marsalis to wreak their damage in the soft under-belly of the music. The basically young audience, enraptured as the competitive element was escalated by all three musicians, came to its feet and afforded the type of reception only rarely experienced at jazz events.

Gillespie made no secret of his delight. He acknowledged the cheers with a beaming smile, and it was as if he was saying that it had been a long journey from Cheraw, South Carolina, but a worthwhile one. This observer found himself thinking back rather less far, not to the countless times he had seen Gillespie work, but to the events that, two hours earlier, had preceded this magnificent concert.

Before the start Gillespie, one of the most important musicians in jazz history, had not been secreted away in his dressing room in the company of various 'minders'. He had been side stage, talking to stage hands and admirers and greeting old friends. Drummer Ben Riley was just one who had passed by *knowing* that he would be well received, and this despite the fact that Gillespie was just about to go out and perform.

Such confidence would be misplaced with many other jazzmen, but John Birks Gillespie has always been a people's champion. He is one of the greatest trumpeters of all time, but he has always been approachable. In 1988 he remains a figure revered throughout the world as an ambassador for his country and for the music he loves. His contribution to that music has been inestimable, and he has done so much more than survive in one of the hardest professions in the world.

DISCOGRAPHICAL ESSAY

Dizzy Gillespie's recording career spans fifty years and has embraced a wide variety of styles. He played a brilliant part in some of the most important records in jazz history, although a less than honest picture of his talent would be painted if recordings doing less than justice to his massive talent were not acknowledged.

His recording debut was on 17 May 1937 with the Teddy Hill band which he had just joined. He was very much influenced by trumpeter Roy Eldridge at the time and although the significance of his *King Porter Stomp* performance (Teddy Hill/Willie Bryant – RCA LPM 10116), is discussed in Chapter One, he was still an aspiring big band trumpeter.

This musical stance was endorsed by his move to the Cab Calloway Orchestra in 1939 and by titles like *Bye Bye Blues* (Cab Calloway – *Penguin Swing* – Jazz Archives JA-8). These were, in the main, conservative performances and bore few traces of the eccentricities that marked his immediately later work. Certainly Gillespie's own opinion of such titles must be rated as being somewhat at odds with the facts, since he felt that they were, in many ways, revolutionary. Even allowing for the advantage of hindsight, one would be pressed to claim that his two choruses on *Bye Bye* had advanced the trumpet in the evolutionary sense.

In contrast, the guest performances made at the same time with Lionel Hampton had a distinctly more liberated air. The vibraphonist has always held that *Hot Mallets* (Lionel Hampton – Hamp the Champ – RCA (Eu) CL89806) contained the first stirrings of bebop. Certainly Gillespie's quirky rhythmic accentation and, for the period, unusual note placings would seem to have moved the music some distance from his orthodox swing band work. In conscience, it must be seen as playing that was based on an established tradition, even if it had offered something of a break-through in the search for greater freedom.

Of more historical significance were the private records of Jerry Newman, recorded at New York's Uptown House in 1941. Considerable confusion still remains about the musicians involved but Gillespie's presence on certain titles is indisputable. Unfortunately, items such as *Kerovac* (Esoteric ESJ 4) exposed as many uncertainties as they did quality moments. The fact that the trumpeter was undoubtedly experimenting with new ideas was obvious but there was a certain lack of confidence on the session recorded and it provided no concrete signpost for the style he was beginning to formulate.

Certainly, his big band records, firstly with Les Hite and then with Lucky Millinder did seem more sure of their stylistic direction. He recorded only four tunes with Millinder but the most outstanding, *Little John Special* (Apollo Jump – Affinity (Eu) AFS 1004), contained two quality blues choruses that attest to his growing confidence and his increasingly impressive instrumental ability.

Gillespie was with the Billy Eckstine Orchestra in 1944. In many ways it was a big band that acted as a forerunner of his own unit. It recorded mainly on National but it was only on the DeLuxe label, early in the band's life that the trumpeter was heard. (*Blowing The Blues Away* – Swingtime ST 1015.) An exciting chase sequence by tenor saxophonists Gene Ammons and Dexter Gordon distinguished the title track *Blowing The Blues Away* but it was on titles like *I Got A Date With Rhythm*, when the whole brass team took its inspiration from Gillespie, or on *Opus X*, when the trumpeter came to the fore, that the band really took off.

In the 1944/45 period, Gillespie began to appear in recording studios with his own small groups. These often teamed him with Charlie Parker and the resulting music was brilliant by any standards. Titles like *Dizzy Atmosphere* and *Shaw 'Nuff* (Groovin' High – Musicraft (Am) MUS 2009) laid the ground rules for bebop. The chord sequence had become the backbone of the style and no longer could the student of jazz speak of 'melodic improvisation'. The harmonic structure had become a building frame and Gillespie was demonstrating just how a new musical edifice could be constructed to accommodate each one. For the newcomer it was perhaps easier to follow when a voice such as that of Sarah Vaughan stood alongside, as it did on *Loverman* (*In The Beginning* – Prestige PR 24030).

In 1945 Gillespie adapted the new music to the big band setting. Sadly the band's life was short but in 1946 he reformed and the unit stayed together until 1950. During that time, it produced some of the most exciting recordings in big band history. It was also at this time that Gillespie's interest in Cuban music took root. He employed conga drum master Chano Pozo and produced a musical fusion that became known as *cubop*. Titles such as *Manteca* and *Cubana Be, Cubana Bop* (1946-49 – RCA NL 89763) were superb examples of the style and with more straight forward tunes such as *Good Bait* and *Minor Walk* (NL 89763) showed how his team of arrangers, including Gil Fuller, John Lewis, Tadd Dameron and George Russell, could create a wedding of traditional sectional interplay, bebop phraseology and make both work better with Cuban flavouring. Outstanding performances on each of the cited titles showed how Gillespie established his own formula for soloing in this then unique musical environment.

The live performance at the Pasadena Civic Auditorium in 1948 perhaps marked the high spot of the band's recorded history. (D.G. Vol 1/2 (1946-48) London ZGL 119.) There the band generated its usual tremendous excitement but significantly the torrid atmosphere was captured on record. Stalwart favourites like *Good Bait* and *One Bass Hit* were given imposing treatment and, although the leader dominated almost every title, it was his investigation of *Round About Midnight* that deserved special mention. The theme's essentially legato nature was ravaged by twelve bars of solo Gillespie trumpet as he challenged its very symmetry, while still making use of the melody's inherent tension as a starting point for his dramatic soliloquy. The mood was momentarily disturbed by a shout from members of the band but the solo was architecturally perfect; as correct in its shape and internal balance as were the carefully composed piano cadenzas of Mozart.

Gillespie's first recording date after the dissolution of the big band in 1950 was with Parker. Produced by Norman Granz it was blighted by the inappropriate choice of Buddy Rich as the drummer. Nevertheless, with the two star soloists together in the studio for the first time since the 1945 Guild session and, with Thelonious Monk and Curly Russell completing the line-up, it could hardly fail. Unfortunately, it was not a session in which Gillespie stood toe to toe with Parker. There were times when his articulation on the faster tunes was imprecise and he was to be heard at his best only when he accepted that he could use his technique to add the improvisation gloss to titles like *Mohawk* and *Leapfrog* (Charlie Parker 1946-54 – Verve (J) OOMJ 3268/77)). Nevertheless, on a title like *Melancholy Baby* his lack of sympathy for the mood of the piece led to less than satisfactory results. It was a performance that perhaps emphasised the one aspect of his style that most changed in the fifties. It was an empty, almost disinterested approach to a pretty ballad but it was an attitude of mind that Gillespie adjusted during the next decade.

No drastic transformation was evident when, later in 1950

Gillespie made his second album with arranger Johnny Richards, using strings and making use of a full twenty five piece orchestra. Gillespie was the only trumpeter, a situation that put him somewhat in isolation, even if it did clarify his position vis a vis the ensemble. On some titles like *Swing Low, Sweet Chariot* (D.G. – *Cool California* – Savoy (Eu) WL 70511 (2)) the strings and the leader sounded as if recorded in different countries. On most of the remainder this was not the case and Richards wisely made no attempt to provide a jazz accented string part. He offered merely a cushion on which the trumpeter was invited to lay his jazz based solo line. On *Alone Together* he played a rather anonymous show-band part but at least it did put the emphasis on good tonal quality. *What Is There To Say*, on the other hand, took him into Hollywood Harry James territory and it was only on *Lullaby Of The Leaves* that the truly crackling bebop horn was heard.

John Coltrane was present on Dee Gee Records' first session, a date that included *Tin Tin Deo* and *Birk's Works* (D.G. – Dee Gee Days – Savoy (Eu) WL 70517 (2)). The saxophonist's contribution was at this stage rather modest but Gillespie, particularly on the twelve bar *Birk's Works*, played with creativity and restraint. The company folded in 1952 but Gillespie, after a solo visit in 1952, went on a European tour in 1953 with a band including Bill Graham on saxes, Wade Legge on piano and with singer Joe Carroll to back up his own vocal efforts. The band's music was effectively documented when a Paris concert was recorded (D.G. *The Complete Pleyel Concert* – Vogue (F) 429002). The short-comings of his colleagues cannot be denied but it was an event strewn with excellent trumpet solos. *The Bluest Blues* and *Birk's Works* left no doubt of his mastery of the modern blues but *My Man* and *I Can't Get Started* gave notice of Gillespie's increasing emotional involvement in ballads of his choice.

On both the 1952 and 1953 trips, Gillespie recorded with an orchestra that he described as operatic strings. Heard in isolation, the twenty five piece units would have had little to recommend them but, on both sessions, the trumpeter was in good lip. The 1952 session (*Dizzy Gillespie And His Operatic Strings Orchestra* – Fontana TL 5343) seemed to emphasize the sighing palm-court aspect of the string work and Gillespie sounded like a lodger in his own house. Nevertheless, his powerfully bluesy trumpet totally dominated both *The Man I Love* and *Sweet and Lovely* and he capped exciting trumpet improvisations with dramatic codas. The string arrangements on the 1953 date (also TL 5343) were more ambitious with the openings of *Pennies From Heaven* and *Jealousy* almost in the Leonard Bernstein manner. Gillespie was unaffected, one way or the other, but his personal contribution to *Stormy Weather* and *I've Got You Under My Skin* were models of brilliant jazz trumpet improvisation.

More significant was the 1953 Massey Hall Concert in Toronto. Chapter Six told of its record doctoring but it was an ad-lib session in which Gillespie, Parker and Powell played superbly well. The sheer fire of the trumpeter's work on *Wee* (*The Quintet Of The Year* – OJC 044) made it the perfect example of up-tempo bop horn playing, while on his well loved *Night In Tunisia* he showed how naturally he could use the strong contours of his own composition to give shape to a solo.

Signing with Norman Granz in 1953 opened many new recording avenues for Gillespie. His first studio session (*Diz and Getz* – Verve (Eu) 2610045) found him with a superb rhythm section but in the unlikely company of Stan Getz, doyen of the cool school. In fact, titles such as *It Don't Mean A Thing* and the twelve bar *Impromptu* were set up to favour the trumpeter. In choosing up-tempo challenges, Gillespie was providing his own bat, his own ball, as well as his own playing surface. Certainly such material did not serve the tenor man's style, based as it was on a thoughtful improvisation process, blessed with effortless grace. It was perhaps inevitable that, in trying to match Gillespie in such circumstances, Getz often sounded pedestrian.

There were certainly more suitable partnerships on offer. Typical was a title as *Birk's Work* (JATP – The Exciting Battle – Pablo 2310 713) recorded live in Stockholm in 1955. Peterson, Brown, Ellis and Bellson, a superb rhythm team, were on hand to generate immense swing. Tenor saxophonist, Flip Phillips picked up the mood, trombonist Bill Harris maintained the impetus and Eldridge cut loose to set up what, for Gillespie, was a masterpiece of a solo. It had everything, speed of execution, total creative intent, a well judged sense of dynamics and, most positively, a feeling of the dramatic.

The two trumpet men met on equally successful terms in the studio. The two sessions that made up *Trumpet Kings* (Verve 2683 022) provided an opportunity to compare them playing together but it also allowed a look at them using the same tune independently. An obvious example was in their individual and personal look at *I'm Thru With Love*. In his 1954 solo Gillespie approached it with a sense of the romantic, there was none of the acidity or boppish angularity that such ballads sometimes encouraged in his playing. Eldridge's 1955 version was equally romantic, attention was paid to relaxation and the use of his musical irascibility kept to a sensible minimum.

In contrast, both men were featured on the 1954 *I Can't Get Started*, both took two choruses and both displayed great sympathy for the theme in hand. This ballad, however, seemed to draw attention to their differences, the busily jagged bop line,

Dizzy with Shorty Rogers and Stan Getz

presenting the antithesis of the slurring more legato approach of the swing era story teller. The same gulf occurred on the up-tempo twelve bar *Trumpet Blues* but it did not stop the two protaganists playing brief, but effective, counterpoint and indulging in some four bar chasing that made nonsense of any stylistic barriers, imagined or real.

A recording that, on paper, found Gillespie in less auspicious company was *One Night In Washington* (D.G. – Elektra Musician 96-0300-1). Complaining to broadcaster Willis Conover about lack of opportunities to work with a big band, the trumpeter was invited to pit his wits against THE Orchestra, a highly impressive rehearsal band based in Washington D.C. As part of the programme, they performed Gillespie's *Afro Suite* a seventeen minute, four part opus that had, not without reason, been originally called the *Manteca Suite*. The charts had been sent on in advance but only limited rehearsal time was available. Nevertheless, the band equitted itself with distinction and the principal was in immaculate form. THE Orchestra were, in fact, more enamoured of the Count Basie style at the time and it was instructive to hear the remainder of the concert during which the Buster Harding-type arrangements of *Hobnail Boogie* and *Wild Bill's Boogie* elicited uncompromisingly boppish trumpet solos that were models of tension building and composition carrying.

The mid fifties were a time of silly, if not actually, damaging album titles. *The Greatest Trumpet Of Them All* (D.G. – Verve 2304 382) was an unfortunate choice if only because it stated what was, in some respects, the obvious. In practice, Gillespie's playing on the 1957 date was surprisingly circumspect. With a superb octet including Benny Golson (tenor), Gigi Gryce (alto) and Ray Bryant (piano), Gillespie made what was an understated but thoroughly involved record. His two smouldering blues choruses on *Blues After Dark* underlined this but the whole album evinced a feeling of emotional commitment. On the melancholy *Sea Breeze* he played in the more overtly romantic manner that he addressed to his 'with strings' sessions but his desire to communicate on titles like *Reminiscing* and *Just By Myself* came across strongly.

The inanity of a title like *Have Trumpet, Will Excite* (D.G. – Verve (J) MV 2696) needs little discussion. The record, made over two days in 1959, however, was a very different matter. Only 'head' arrangements were used but Gillespie's masterly treatment of *My Heart Belongs To Daddy* and his buoyant stroll with *My Man* had the assurance of well prepared material. The session highlight was the old war horse *St Louis Blues*, distinguished by Junior Mance's rolling piano solo but significant for the way in which the master's tightly muted solo over-rode the easy Latinish gait of the piece.

The 1960 album, *A Portrait Of Duke Ellington* (D.G. – Verve MGV 8356) was an important statement of where Gillespie stood in relation to his fellow trumpeters of the period. The significance of arranger Clare Fischer's thinking is outlined in Chapter Eight but *Concerto For Cootie* remained the standout title.

Inevitably his working group produced more casual records. *An Electrifying Evening With The Dizzy Gillespie Quintet* (D.G. – Verve (J) MV 2605) was typical and it presented the trumpeter in a very relaxed mood. On *Kush* and *Salt Peanuts* he seemed casual to the brink of carelessness but it was such spontaneous attitudes that made this record an object lesson in Gillespie lore and a perfect example of a player thinking on his feet, while still giving his solos shape and coherence.

Argentinian Lalo Schifrin was not the ideal pianist for the quintet but, as the bossa nova rhythms of *Desafinado* and the Brazilian manner of *Pau De Arara* (D.G. – *Oo Pop a Da* – Affinity AFF 142) showed, his light dancing figures could be of use if the material was right. Deficiences were only really evident on a title like *Kush*, from the same 1961 Monterey Jazz Festival set, and then because Gillespie's trumpet set up an energy field that needed complementing with power from the piano stool.

Where Schifrin did contribute most positively was in his composing and arranging. *Gillespiana* was premiered at Carnegie Hall in November 1961 but it was *The New Continent*, commissioned for the 1962 Monterey Festival, that was the more radical item. (*Dizzy Gillespie And The Big Band – 1965* – Trip TLP 5584.) Despite the title, it was recorded in 1962 and it turned out to be a superb showcase for Gillespie. It received a mixed, critical reaction when it first appeared and observers, suspicious of any descriptive jazz work, found it too formal. In fact, it was in no way programmatic and it was never Schifrin's intention that it should be. The composer set out to use elements from the music of Spain, Africa and America and the sympathy with which Gillispie responded indicated that there was a strong rapport between the two men. Occasionally the ensemble was ponderous but Gillespie's delightful solo on *Conquerors* and on the waltz-time *Empire* showed his ease with the material, even if it was the 'theme and improvisation' atmosphere of *Swords* that drew his most natural response. Having said this, it is important to judge the whole work as an entity and not merely as a showcase for the trumpeter. As such, it was thematically imaginative, with *Conquerors* its most melodic theme and *Chorale* the most complex section in a work that stood strangely apart from the main body of Gillespie's recorded output.

In total contrast, the poorest of his sixties recordings were assembled on *Souled Out* (D.G. – Pye PKL 4403), an anthology with mixed personnels, each setting out to present Gillespie as a 'soul' product. If only because of its aesthetic poverty, it is an essential record in a full appreciation of the trumpeter's career and was, not for the last time, a chance to hear him playing out of position.

How much more appropriate to hear him in his natural habitat – the big band. 1968 saw him working with what was dubbed the Reunion Big Band. Recorded live at the Berlin Jazz Festival (D.G. – *20th And 30th Anniversary* – MPS 15207) it had a superb eight man brass team that effectively inspired Gillespie to his finest work. After the audience had responded to the superbly shouting brass work on *Things To Come*, Gillespie remarked that it 'sounded like a real band'. In this stunning understatement was the reason for the trumpeter's ease with the idiom. Picking his way through the rifle crack punctuation of a crack trumpet team had always stimulated him. Some men might be daunted by such 'support' but, as *One Bass Hit* and *Things Are Here* showed, this supremely confident man took inspiration from it. The quality of the reed section was the final icing on the cake and their work on titles like *Fresco* completed an outstanding record that was undoubtedly by a real 'real band'.

Early in 1971, a delightful quintet record with Dixielander Bobby Hackett sired titles like *Love For Sale, Jitterbug Waltz* and *Willow Weep For Me* (*The Great Modern Jazz Trumpet-Festival* (EV 215)) but his brilliant and more natural form of small group expression was captured on a two album set that chronicled the superb Giants of Jazz Sextets concerts in Japan and England (*Giants of Jazz* – Atlantic SD2-905). These were uniformly excellent, although a special mention should be made of Gillespie's playing on *Night In Tunisia*, where he still managed to sound inspired on a title he must have been able to play in his sleep.

Very little that Gillespie has ever played sounds perfunctory, however, and his superb contribution to the Radio City Music Hall concert in 1972 seemed to vindicate George Wein's decision to revamp the Newport Festival as a New York City event. (*Newport In New York '72* – Atlantic ATL 40446.) On *Bag's Groove* his open horned shout took the theme by the throat as he pranced across Max Roach's dancing drum figures, while on *Tunisia* he did it again, transforming a potentially hackneyed vehicle into a simple prop for a joyful trumpet extravaganza.

Gillespie's return to the Norman Granz stable could hardly have had a more auspicious start (*Dizzy Gillespie's Big Four* – Pablo 2310 719). The big three working with the trumpeter were guitarist Joe Pass, bassist Ray Brown and drummer Mickey Roker and a fine group they made. Listening to Pass' supple figures behind the muted trumpet solo on *Frelimo*, to Brown's walking bass behind its poignant opening to *Russian Lullaby* or to Roker's old world propulsiveness behind the cohesive solo on *Bebop* was enough to make one appreciate that such music was beyond stylistic barriers.

Similar astylistic atmospheres prevailed when he made outstanding albums with Machito (D.G. – *Afro-Cuban Jazz Moods* – Pablo 2310 771), with Eldridge and blues shouter Joe Turner (*The Trumpet Kings Meet Joe Turner* – Pablo 2310 717) and with altoist Benny Carter (*Carter Gillespie Inc.* – Pablo 2310 781). All three maintained consistent standards but of special interest in a different way was his 1976 *Dizzy's Party* (Pablo 2310 784). In terms of Gillespie's finest work it was unquestionably second class, although the reasons for its shortcomings were illuminating. It would be too glib to dismiss it as commercial and, in introducing the Brazilian rhythms of Paulinho Da Costa, he could have said to be on familiar ground. The fault, if any, lay with Gillespie himself. In setting out to produce a 'dance' album he seemed prepared to accept any available rhythmic gait. His solo never took over against the general clutter of *Dizzy's Party*, while on *Harlem Samba* his well wrought boppish lines seemed to have no connection with the four man rhythm team or with the Roland Kirkish flute solo by Ray Pizza that followed.

In contrast, Gillespie's first record with his protege Jon Faddis (*Dizzy Gillespie Jam, Montreux '77* – Pablo 2308 211) was a tremendous success. Few would deny their similarities but, as a shapely ballad like *Girl Of My Dreams* showed, Gillespie's verbosity had a more contained feeling to it. Faddis essayed the same arpeggiated territory but, at that time, seemed more self consciously dramatic. *Get Happy* demonstrated his technical mastery and, if the Gillespie solo exhibited greater maturity, there was a more than thirty five year age gap to ensure that this should be so.

Gillespie loved the challenge of fellow trumpeters and a somewhat unusual album of rejected takes teamed him with two of the finest. The 1980 *Alternative Blues* (Pablo 2310 136) with Clark Terry and Freddie Hubbard contained four takes of the title track. Confusion in the rhythm section had made the takes necessary but, whatever the reason, it provided a chance to hear the way in which Gillespie used the same framework, while allowing his improvisational ideas to change the complexion of each solo. More significantly, it showed that at this stage of his career he concerned himself far more with content than with decoration. This aspect was further highlighted when set against the spectacular but somewhat superficial trumpet work of Arturo Sandoval who, in 1982, recorded with Gillespie and a Scandinavian rhythm section (D.G. – *To A Finland Station* – Pablo 2310 889).

Considering that Gillespie had passed his sixtieth birthday by some distance, his playing in the eighties remained, in the main, technically secure. Fragile moments tended to occur when his heart was not in a project and so it appeared with *Closer To The Source* (D.G. – Atlantic (Eu) 781 646-1) recorded in 1984. Sidemen Branford Marsalis, Stevie Wonder, Kenny Kirkland and Mino Cinelu acquit themselves well enough but Gillespie's playing on *Could It Be You* should have guaranteed that it ended in the mixing room waste bin. His playing was hardly better on the remaining tunes and on *Its Time For Love* and *Just Before Dawn* one can almost sense the apathy.

Considering the undoubted quality of his playing outside the studio, his collaboration with singer Lilian Terry (*Oo-Shoo-Be-*

Doo-Bee – Soul Note SN 1147) in 1985 was similarly disappointing. Only on the unusually gentle paced *Con Alma* did he stretch out and even then there were barren parts to his solo.

Newcomers to Gillespie's music would be well advised to look back to earlier triumphs, although it must be hoped that some of his magnificent playing in the 1987 Festivals will find its way into record.

BIBLIOGRAPHY

Barnett, Anthony	*Don Byas; Tenor Saxophone* (Jazz Monthly September 1965)
Berendt, Joachim	*The Jazz Book* (St Albans: Paladin, 1976)
Bruyninckx, W.	*Bebop, Hard Bop, West Coast Vol 1-6* (Discography)
Burns, Jim	*The Billy Eckstine Band* (Jazz Monthly January 1968)
	Dizzy Gillespie: The Early 1950s Part One (Jazz Journal International January 1969)
	Dizzy Gillespie: The Early 1950s Part Two (Jazz Journal International February 1969)
	Dizzy Gillespie: 1945-50 (Jazz Journal International January 1972)
	Early Birks (Jazz Journal International March 1971)
	Lesser Known Bands of the Forties: Dizzy Gillespie and Gil Fuller (Jazz Monthly March 1969)
Case, Brian/Stan Britt	*The Illustrated Encyclopedia of Jazz* (London: Salamander Books, 1978)
Chilton, John	*Who's Who of Jazz* (London: Macmillan, 1985 and New York: Da Capo Press Inc, 1985)
Condon, Eddie, ed.	*Eddie Condon's Treasury of Jazz* (New York: 1956)
Feather, Leonard	*The Encyclopedia of Jazz* (London: Arthur Baker, 1961)
	From Satchmo to Miles (New York: 1972)

Feather, Leonard and Ira Gitler	*The Encyclopedia of Jazz in the Seventies* (London: Quartet Books Ltd, 1978)
Gardner, Mark	*Dizzy's (back in) Business* (Jazz Journal International October 1968)
Gibson, Frank	*The Billy Eckstine Band* (Jazz Journal International May 1970)
Gibson, Michael	*Big Band Jazz* (Jazz Journal International January 1960)
Gillespie, Dizzy with Al Fraser	*Dizzy – To Be Or Not To Bop* (Garden City, New York: 1979, London: W. H. Allen, 1980, and Quartet Books, 1982)
Gitler, Ira	*Jazz Masters of the Forties* (New York: Macmillan Publishing, 1966 and London: Collier MacMillan Publishers, 1966)
Gleason, Ralph J.	*Celebrating the Duke, and Louis, Bessie, Billie, Bird, Carmen, Miles, Dizzy and Other Heroes* (Boston and Toronto: 1975)
Hennessey, Mike	*Dizzy Gillespie: the Greatest Trumpet of Them All* (Jazz Journal International July 1984)
Hoefer, George	*The Big Bands: the Glorious Dizzy Gillespie Orchestra* (Down Beat August 1966)
Horricks, Raymond	*Dizzy Gillespie* (Tunbridge Wells: Spellmount Ltd, 1984 and New York: Hippocrene Books Inc, 1984) *Dizzy Gillespie and the Be-bop Revolution* (New York: 1984)
James, Michael	*Dizzy Gillespie* (London: Cassell & Co, 1959)
Jepsen, Jørgen Grunnet	*A Discography of Dizzy Gillespie* (Copenhagen: 1969)
McCarthy, Albert J.	*The Big Band Era: Cab Calloway* (Jazz Monthly November 1960)
McCarthy, Albert J. Alun Morgan, Paul Oliver and Max Harrison	*Jazz on Record* (London: Hanover Books, 1968)
McRae, Barry	*A. B. Basics: Dizzy Gillespie* (Jazz Journal International September 1969)

Morgan, Alun	*Review of: 'To Be Or Not To Bop' by Dizzy Gillespie and Al Frazer* (Jazz Journal International June 1980)
Morgan, Alun, and Raymond Horricks	*Modern Jazz* (London: Victor Gollancz Ltd, 1958)
Peterson, Owen	*The Massey Hall Concert* (Jazz Journal International March 1970)
Russell, Ross	*Bird Lives* (London: Quartet Books, 1973)
Shaw, John	*Kenny Clarke* (Jazz Journal International October 1969)
Shera, Michael	*The Billy Eckstine Band* (Jazz Journal International November 1960)
Travis, Dempsey	*An Autobiography of Black Jazz* (Chicago: 1983)
Woolley, Stan	*Dizzy Gillespie: Reflections On Bebop* (Jazz Journal International June 1976)

INDEX

132

135